RANGER
HANDBOOK

Military Strategies, Survival Techniques, and Leadership — Everything a Ranger Needs to Know to Successfully Overcome Any Challenge

TACTICAL OPS INSTITUTE

DOWNLOAD YOUR FREE BONUS NOW!

We have some exclusive bonus materials for you as a way of saying thank you and to further enhance your experience. These extras include:

- **BONUS 1: Operation Preparation Checklist**
- **BONUS 2: Medical Emergency Management Checklist**
- **BONUS 3: Emergency Situations Checklist**

To claim these valuable resources go to:

https://micolipublishing.wixsite.com/ranger

TABLE OF CONTENT

CHAPTER 1: CORE CONCEPTS OF COMMAND

HISTORYCAL CHRONICLES OF RANGERS

The narrative of the American Rangers captures the spirit of resilience and leadership over decades of armed conflict. Rangers have carved a path of bravery and strategic prowess through colonial battles and modern conflicts, molding the very core of military command and elite operations.

Ranger history begins in the stormy environments of early America. During King Philip's War in 1675, Benjamin Church's Company of Independent Rangers laid the groundwork for unconventional warfare with successful attacks against hostile foes. This early Ranger force demonstrated the blending of traditional frontier abilities with structured military operations, laying the groundwork for a doctrine that would grow significantly over the decades.

Major Robert Rogers codified these procedures in 1756, when he formed nine Ranger companies to service during the French and Indian War. Rogers' Rangers, known for their tough discipline and mastery of guerrilla tactics, grew into a formidable force, applying concepts that have since become fundamental Ranger doctrine. Their methods of operation stressed mobility, surprise, and intimate terrain knowledge—principles that still inspire Ranger tactics today.

The Revolutionary War also saw the emergence of Ranger tactics under leaders like Colonel Daniel Morgan, whose unit, Morgan's Riflemen, became famous for their sharpshooting abilities. Another prominent character, Francis Marion, sometimes known as the "Swamp Fox," used the deep Carolina swamps to his advantage, coordinating guerilla attacks that hindered British operations while considerably aiding the American cause.

As the country grew and new problems arose, the notion of Rangers was examined and altered. During the American Civil War, individuals such as John S. Mosby, who headed Mosby's Rangers, used their extensive knowledge of local topography to perform quick strikes while evading bigger enemy forces.

Major William O. Darby formed the 1st Ranger Battalion in 1942, ushering in a substantial rebirth and expansion of the Rangers. This unit, made up of chosen volunteers, demonstrated Ranger bravery during the Dieppe Raid and in important actions throughout North Africa, Sicily, and Italy. Their daring in battle cemented the Rangers' reputation as an elite unit capable of carrying out the most difficult missions behind enemy lines.

The Rangers' legacy extended beyond the European Theater. In the Pacific, the 6th Ranger Battalion carried out some of the most daring operations of the war, including the release of POWs from the Cabanatuan prison camp in the Philippines, which is now regarded as one of the most heroic moments in military history.

Following WWII, the Korean War saw the activation of Ranger formations such as the 8th Army Ranger Company, which excelled in deep penetration raids and joint operations, setting new benchmarks for operational excellence. The Vietnam War increased the scope of Ranger missions by establishing long-range reconnaissance patrols, which were eventually organized as the 75th Ranger Regiment. These groups specialized in direct action and reconnaissance, which were crucial in counterinsurgency and unconventional warfare.

The reactivation of Ranger battalions in the 1970s under General Creighton Abrams signaled a new revival of Ranger capabilities. The formation of the 75th Ranger Regiment in 1986 standardized the structure and roles of modern Ranger units, stressing adaptability, rapid response, and high-impact operations.

Rangers have played critical roles in operations dating back to Panama in 1989 and the ongoing Global War on Terror. Their responsibilities have grown beyond traditional fighting to encompass nation-building and counter-terrorism, reflecting the changing dynamics of modern warfare, in which strategic thought, agility, and tactical competence are essential.

The Rangers' enduring culture, expressed in their motto "Rangers Lead the Way," emphasizes their devotion to leadership, quality, and the unwavering pursuit of mission success in the face of enormous obstacles. As we reflect on the Rangers' illustrious history, it is apparent that it is about more than only the wars fought and won, but also about the evolution of tactical leadership and the indomitable spirit that distinguishes every Ranger.

The Rangers' heritage exemplifies the value of competent leadership and an unrelenting search of perfection. It serves as a solid pillar for comprehending the fundamental notions of command and is a constant source of motivation for those who wish to lead in the face of adversity.

FUNDAMENTAL PRINCIPLES OF COMMAND

Leadership inside the Rangers involves more than just holding a position; it is primarily about inspiring and guiding others to reach larger organizational goals. This unique talent separates Army leaders who, through their duties or specified responsibilities, move their teams above the routine to exceptional achievement.

Ranger leadership is based on the dual duty for mission success and the well-being of subordinates. Leaders in this elite group are tasked with developing their units into competent and cohesive teams capable of operating smoothly in high-pressure situations. A leader's performance is judged not just by their ability to issue instructions, but also by their ability to create an environment in which each team member is motivated and prepared to contribute optimally to the unit's goals.

The three fundamental pillars of Ranger leadership—purpose, direction, and tenacity—are woven into the fabric of daily tasks and strategic decisions.

- The purpose gives the team a clear objective and grasp of the bigger picture of their mission. This clarity is essential not only in combat situations, but also in training and preparation, when each activity is strategically important.
- Direction from leaders ensures that all team efforts are coordinated and aligned with the unit's objectives. It entails defining clear, achievable goals and then preparing and allocating resources to attain them. Effective direction eliminates misallocation of effort and keeps the team's energies focused on key tasks.
- The Rangers tenacity in the face of adversity stems from their strong motivation. A motivated Ranger is inspired by a sense of duty, pride in their role, and faith in their superiors' judgments. Leaders inspire their teams by setting a good example through their behaviors, attitudes, and dedication.

Balancing and Maximizing Operational Elements: Maneuver, Firepower, and Protection

A Ranger leader's tactical acumen is demonstrated by their ability to balance and utilize the three vital elements of battle power: maneuverability, firepower, and protection. Maneuver is the planned movement of forces to obtain a tactical advantage, whereas firepower is the deployment of weapon systems to deliver effective force against the opponent. Protection refers to the efforts used to maintain the force's fighting capability.

Each element must be precisely calibrated based on the mission's specific requirements. For example, in a reconnaissance mission, stealth (a form of maneuver) takes precedence, lowering the need for firepower to escape discovery. In contrast, in a direct assault, firepower may be maximized to quickly destroy threats, while high mobility ensures rapid advance and little exposure to enemy attacks.

In essence, the Rangers' leadership style is defined by a thorough comprehension of these concepts, which are implemented through the prism of experience and tactical knowledge. Leaders are expected to make judgments that not only attempt to achieve immediate goals, but also anticipate and minimize prospective difficulties, so protecting their troops and assuring mission success even in the most difficult circumstances.

As we learn more about the roles and responsibilities of Rangers leaders, it becomes evident that these core principles are more than just theoretical concepts; they are lived experiences that shape the Ranger community's character.

Attributes Necessary for Effective Leadership

Effective leadership in the Rangers is dependent not only on tactical and technical proficiency, but also on essential personal characteristics that instill confidence and respect. These characteristics are crucial in determining a leader's capacity to effectively manage both people and situations.

- **Character**: A Ranger leader's character is built on Army principles such as loyalty, responsibility, respect, selfless service, honor, integrity, and personal courage. These qualities, combined with empathy for subordinates and steadfast discipline, produce a leadership model that is both formidable and honorable. Empathy enables commanders to understand and regard the welfare of their troops, building a culture of mutual respect. Discipline ensures that they maintain standards and effectiveness even in the most stressful situations.

- **Presence**: A leader's presence is a combination of military and professional appearance, physical condition, and confidence. Resilience, an important part of a Ranger's presence, ensures that commanders can withstand physical and psychological trials while providing a stern example for their soldiers. During times of uncertainty and crisis, soldiers often look to their leaders for stability and assurance.
- **Intellect**: Intellectual capability in leadership encompasses more than just cognitive abilities. It involves mental agility, which enables leaders to think critically and adapt in rapidly changing environments. Sound judgment, imaginative problem-solving, interpersonal tact, and extensive knowledge of military tactics and strategy are all necessary. These intellectual traits enable leaders to create successful strategies and make judgments that foresee and reduce risks while increasing mission accomplishment.

Key Competencies for Ranger Leaders

The Rangers' leadership competencies are designed to meet the challenges of both conventional and unconventional warfare, ensuring that leaders can effectively function within and influence both their immediate and broader organizational structures.

- Oath to the Constitution and Adherence to Laws: The commitment to upholding the Constitution and obeying civilian authorities serves as the legal and moral foundation for military service. This commitment assures that Ranger operations are consistent with national principles and legal standards, which strengthens the legitimacy and accountability of military actions.
- Combat Power Dynamics: Ranger commanders must understand the dynamics of fighting power, namely how to develop, apply, and sustain it. This ability entails not only the tactical use of force, but also the strategic management of resources and personnel in order to maximize combat effectiveness. Leaders must be competent at combining these factors in order to maximize their force's operational performance.
- Influence on Leadership: Leadership impact can take both positive and harmful aspects. Positively, it entails inspiring and motivating troops to give their all through exemplary behavior and proactive involvement. Negatively, it might result from coercion or abuse of authority, eroding trust and morale. Recognizing and fostering the appropriate balance of influence is critical to sustaining a healthy, successful command climate.

Leadership in the Rangers is context-driven and dynamic, adapting to shifting degrees of responsibility and the particular needs of each mission. This adaptable methodology ensures that Ranger commanders are effective not only in direct combat, but also in larger organizational and situational contexts. Ranger leaders ensure their teams are capable, cohesive, and ready to face any challenge by constantly strengthening these qualities and skills, embodying the notion of "Rangers lead the way."

Levels of Leadership

- **Direct Leadership**: This is the most immediate level of leadership, in which leaders are actively involved in their teams on the ground. Tactical maneuvers, direct combat engagements, and small unit crises all include the immediate and tangible application of leadership qualities. Leaders at this level must be capable of making quick decisions that are critical to the safety and performance of their teams.
- **Organizational Leadership**: Leaders at this level manage larger units and must traverse more difficult

operational conditions. They are in charge of strategic planning and resource management, ensuring that their decisions align with overall corporate goals. These leaders shape the structure, readiness, and strategic direction of their units, necessitating a thorough understanding of both military doctrine and organizational dynamics.

- **Situational Leadership**: This style is critical in operations with variable factors where decisions must adapt to changing conditions. Situational leaders must excel in adaptability and resilience, knowing when to change tactics and command approaches based on real-time information. This level focuses on integrating intelligence, soldier capabilities, and mission objectives to dynamically lead operations toward success.

Special Leadership Conditions

- **Formal vs. Informal Leadership**: Formal leadership roles are identified by rank and official posts in the military hierarchy, such as PLs or PSGs. Informal leadership, on the other hand, arises as a result of a soldier's competence and esteem among peers, often exerting influence beyond their official authority.
- **Collective Leadership**: In some cases, leadership responsibilities are shared by a group rather than a single person. This strategy, which draws on the combined skills and insights of multiple leaders to develop strategies and carry out operations, is especially effective in complicated or confusing situations.
- **Situational Dynamics**: These occur when unanticipated changes in the mission environment force leaders to quickly adapt their command technique. Leaders must be skilled at managing the stress of the unknown and guiding their staff through the unexpected obstacles that can arise in every operation.

Leadership in Action: Roles and Responsibilities

Effective leadership within the Rangers is characterized by clear roles and responsibilities that anchor the unit's operations.

Platoon Leader (PL)

- *Operational Command*: The PL is ultimately responsible for all areas of the platoon's activities. This comprises mission strategic planning and tactical execution, which require recognizing the platoon's strengths and effectively deploying them against the opponent.
- *Development and Training*: Beyond combat, a platoon leader is in charge of the platoon's training and growth, ensuring that all members are proficient in their jobs and prepared for the difficulties that await them in the field.
- *Communication and Decision-Making*: The PL's primary responsibility is to ensure clear and consistent communication with both upper leadership and subordinate troops. Effective decision-making, based on thorough situational awareness, is critical to mission accomplishment.

Platoon Sergeant (PSG)

- *Advisory Role*: The PSG acts as the senior advisor to the PL, providing insights and recommendations that are crucial for operational planning and decision-making.
- *Logistics and Administration*: Managing the logistical and administrative aspects of platoon operations, including supplies, equipment, and personnel management, falls under the PSG's responsibilities.
- *Operational Oversight*: The PSG ensures that all orders and plans are executed efficiently, supervising the implementation and adjusting as necessary to support the PL's strategy. They also contribute significantly to the platoon's morale and discipline.

Squad Leader (SL)

- *Tactical Leadership and Oversight*: The Squad Leader is responsible for providing direct tactical direction and oversight to their squad. This position necessitates a thorough awareness of both the mission objectives and the specific capabilities of squad members. The SL must transform strategic orders into clear, actionable tasks that can be carried out in combat.
- *Discipline and Readiness*: The SL's key responsibilities include maintaining discipline and ensuring operational readiness. This includes conducting frequent assessments on squad members' physical and mental condition to ensure they are always battle-ready. The SL also develops a sense of resilience and togetherness, which are essential in high-stress situations.

Weapons Squad Leader (WSL)

- *Control of Firepower*: The Weapons Squad Leader manages and deploys the unit's heavy weaponry. This position is crucial in establishing strategic weapon locations that can significantly impact combat dynamics.
- *Tactical Employment*: The WSL collaborates closely with the SL to smoothly incorporate the heavy weapons into the unit's overall tactical maneuvers. This entails planning the best use of weaponry based on topography, adversary posture, and mission goals, guaranteeing maximum effectiveness while minimizing risk to the unit.

Team Leader (TL)

- *Direct Action and Control*: Team Leaders oversee smaller sections of the team, directly regulating movements and actions during operations. They are critical in guiding their troops across risky terrain, coordinating movements with other teams, and carrying out complex sections of the operations plan.
- *Security and Tactical Enforcement*: TL guarantees that all security measures are followed throughout missions. They are also in charge of enforcing tactical operations, ensuring that all team members understand their roles and do them to the best of their abilities. This is critical not just for mission accomplishment, but also for the safety of the team.

Support Roles and Their Impact on Leadership

Support duties within Ranger units, while not often at the forefront of combat, are critical to maintaining the functionality and success of missions. These positions provide critical services that allow the combat arms to carry out their duty efficiently.

Medic

- *Health and Combat Readiness*: Medics are responsible for the Rangers' health and medical readiness. This involves routine medical checkups, emergency medical care, and planning for a swift medical response in the event of a casualty.
- *Direct Support and CASEVAC*: Medics in the field provide direct help during combat operations. They are prepared to perform under duress, giving essential medical interventions that can save lives. Medics also coordinate CASEVAC (casualty evacuation), a critical duty that includes planning and carrying out the extraction of injured soldiers.

Radio Operator

- *Communication Maintenance*: Radio operators guarantee that all communication connections within the unit and with higher command are operational and secure. This function is crucial, particularly in operations that rely significantly on real-time information transmission.

- *Operational Security and Coordination*: Radio Operators contribute to the protection of operational plans and troop movements against hostile detection by maintaining secure and effective communications. Their ability to manage communications influences the unit's ability to respond to changing battlefield conditions and leadership orders.

CHAPTER 2: OPERATIONAL STRATEGIES

GUIDELINES FOR COMMANDING FORCES

Effective tactical preparation and execution are important to the success of infantry operations, particularly in the Rangers, where accuracy and agility are essential. The process begins with a deep grasp of the mission, which informs all future strategic decisions and actions. Leaders assess the mission's objectives, enemy capabilities, and available resources, laying the groundwork for subsequent tactical preparation and execution. This early stage of planning is critical because it establishes the strategic framework for the operation.

As the strategy is put into action, the execution phase examines its practical applicability against the dynamic and often unpredictable backdrop of conflict. Rangers view execution as more than just following predetermined strategies; it also includes responding to changing battlefield situations, making quick judgments, and revising tactics as needed. Successful military operations are distinguished by their ability to seamlessly integrate planning and execution, making adjustments in response to immediate tactical needs and unforeseen problems. It guarantees that operations are both flexible and responsive, allowing for maximum mission success while maintaining operational tempo. In this way, the abilities and understanding of tactical planning and execution are important, allowing Rangers to effectively lead, manage, and react in complicated combat scenarios.

The Troop Leading Procedures (TLP)

In the demanding environment of Ranger operations, the Troop Leading Procedures (TLP) serve as the foundation for planning and carrying out missions with precision and speed. These protocols ensure that every Ranger leader, from novice officers to seasoned commanders, takes a systematic approach to mission planning and execution, increasing the likelihood of success in diverse and difficult combat circumstances.

The procedure begins when a mission is received, indicating the start of a critical period. Leaders evaluate the urgency and intricacy of the orders, which might range from routine operations to quick reaction missions that require immediate action. The initial receipt of the mission establishes the overall operational tempo and dictates the next phases in the TLP.

Following mission receipt, it is critical to issue a warning order. This initial instruction, which is often concise yet detailed, describes the mission's core features. It gives enough information for subunits to begin their preliminary operations immediately. The warning order usually follows the five-paragraph operations order structure, which ensures uniformity and clarity in communication at all levels of command.

As the planning phase begins, leaders draft a preliminary strategy based on a thorough mission analysis. This contains an analysis of the task using the METT-TC framework. This paradigm promotes a comprehensive understanding of the operational environment and the work at hand.

The following steps are to initiate movement and perform reconnaissance. These actions are interconnected because real-time reconnaissance information can be used to revise or redirect the preliminary plan. This phase is crucial for adapting to ground realities that may not have been completely realized during the early planning stages.

Once the reconnaissance data has been incorporated into the plan, the leader approves the operational strategy and issues the operations order. This order summarizes the entire plan, ensuring that all subunits are completely aware of their duties, objectives, and expectations. The clarity of this order is critical to ensure cohesive and synchronized behavior among the unit's many components.

The TLP's final step is the supervision and refining phase. During this stage, leaders supervise the preparation for war through extensive rehearsals and inspections. These activities are intended to discover any differences or potential flaws with the plan, allowing for revisions before the operation goes live. Rehearsals, in particular, serve an important role in ensuring that all units understand their jobs and can perform them flawlessly under duress.

This systematic approach to mission planning and execution is more than just following protocols; it is about instilling in the Rangers a culture of careful preparation, adaptable thinking, and flawless execution. It guarantees that when Rangers are called to action, they are not simply responding to conditions, but are carrying out well-planned strategies that account for every predictable variable in the complicated tapestry of combat operations.

Detailed Planning Techniques

In the challenging realm of Ranger operations, mission analysis and task identification are two important components that serve as the foundation for successful mission planning and execution. These techniques are strongly embedded in the Rangers' leadership fabric, demonstrating a systematic approach to combat preparedness and strategic deployment.

Mission Analysis

The first stage in planning for any operation is to do a complete mission analysis. This study is based on the METT-TC framework, which stands for Mission, Enemy, Terrain and Weather, Troops and Support Available, Time Available, and Civil Considerations. Each component of METT-TC is rigorously reviewed to ensure a complete awareness of the operational environment and the parameters within which the Rangers must operate.

- **Mission**: Leaders start by defining the objective clearly. Understanding the mission's purpose guides all strategic decisions and tactical actions.
- **Enemy**: Knowing the enemy's capabilities, likely intentions, and current dispositions allows leaders to anticipate challenges and plan countermeasures effectively.
- **Terrain and Weather**: The geographical topography and weather conditions can have a considerable impact on operations. Leaders analyze these factors to determine the best approaches and tactics suitable for the environment.
- **Troops and Support Available**: Assessing the available manpower and resources, including logistics and reinforcements, enables commanders to allocate resources effectively and efficiently.
- **Time Available**: Time constraints frequently drive the urgency of planning and execution. Effective time management ensures that enough time is spent on planning, preparation, and execution without jeopardizing operational security or effectiveness.
- **Civil Considerations**: Understanding the impact of military operations on the civilian population and vice versa is crucial, especially in conflicts where civilian interaction is high.

Identification of Tasks

After the mission study is complete, the second critical step is to select tasks. This entails distinguishing between specified and implied tasks obtained from the operation orders. Specified tasks are expressly stated in the orders, instructing specific actions necessary to complete the mission. Implied tasks, while not explicitly specified, are required for the mission's successful completion and must be inferred and carried out.

- **Specified Tasks**: These are clear and unambiguous tasks that are directly communicated within the operations order. They form the backbone of the mission's objectives.
- **Implied Tasks**: These tasks require intuitive understanding from leaders. Identifying these tasks involves reading between the lines of the operations order and understanding what must be done to support the specified tasks and overall mission success.
- **Mission Essential Tasks**: Among the identified tasks, certain ones are critical to the mission's success. These mission-critical actions must be prioritized and done flawlessly in order to achieve the intended result.

The process of task identification include not only identifying what needs to be done, but also ranking these tasks based on their importance to the mission. Leaders must ensure that each task is consistent with the overall mission objectives, and that personnel understand their roles and duties. This clarity is critical for sustaining operational coherence and ensuring that all efforts are focused on the same goal.

In summary, careful mission analysis using the METT-TC framework, as well as meticulous job identification, both explicit and implied, are critical for Ranger operation planning and execution. These protocols ensure that Ranger leaders are fully prepared to lead their teams into complicated and tough circumstances, with a well-defined strategy and a thorough awareness of all operational aspects.

GATHERING AND USING COMBAT INTELLIGENCE

In the high-stakes realm of Ranger operations, the ability to properly obtain and use combat intelligence is a vital aspect that can influence the outcome of military conflicts. This chapter delves into the practical aspects of how intelligence is acquired, evaluated, and disseminated to ensure mission success.

Practical Aspects of Combat Intelligence

Combat intelligence collecting is a continual process that has a substantial impact on Ranger operation planning and execution. It entails gathering information about the enemy, the terrain, and other environmental aspects that may influence tactical decisions.

1. **Information Collection Methods**: Rangers use a variety of tactics to gather intelligence, including direct observation, modern surveillance equipment, and reports from local sources or ally forces. This information must be precise and reliable because it serves as the foundation for making sound tactical decisions.

2. **SALUTE Report Format**: Rangers employ the SALUTE format (Size, Activity, Location, Unit/Uniform, Time, and Equipment) as one of their key tools for reporting intelligence in the field. This format helps to standardize reports, ensuring that they are clear, succinct, and complete. For example, observing seven enemy personnel going southwest, dressed in olive-drab uniforms with distinctive insignia and armed with heavy weapons, provides a picture of the threat at a given time and location.

3. **Field Sketches and Maps**: Field sketches, as well as verbal or written reports, are critical components of combat intelligence. These illustrations depict essential tactical characteristics such adversary positions, barriers, and terrain layout. Effective sketches are uncluttered and focus on military significance, which improves knowledge of the operating environment.

4. **Handling of Captured Materials and Prisoners**: The acquisition of intelligence also includes the processing of captured documents and captives. Documents are meticulously labeled with the time and location of capture for future study. In contrast, prisoners are handled in accordance with the Geneva Convention and provide important real-time enemy intelligence.

5. **Debriefing**: Following the mission, a systematic debriefing session is undertaken. This enables the unit to gain insights from a variety of team members, combining direct observations with reported data to construct a complete picture of the opponent and their tactics.

The successful application of battle information not only informs tactical decisions made during an operation, but it also helps with strategic planning for future missions. It enables Ranger troops to adapt to changing battlefield situations, predict enemy moves, and respond accurately. Rangers improve their information collecting skills through rigorous training and real-world application, ensuring that they stay one step ahead of their adversaries.

Practical Examples of Combat Intelligence Use

In this section, we look at concrete examples of how Rangers use combat intelligence techniques effectively in the field. These scenarios highlight the actual use of intelligence collecting and analysis abilities, both of which are vital to Ranger missions.

Example 1: Utilizing the SALUTE Report

During a reconnaissance mission, a Ranger patrol identifies a small enemy unit. Utilizing the SALUTE report format, the patrol leader quickly gathers and disseminates crucial information:

- **Size**: Approximately ten enemy soldiers.

- **Activity**: Digging in and establishing defensive positions.
- **Location**: Wooded area near grid coordinate XY123456.
- **Unit/Uniform**: Soldiers wearing desert camouflage with no visible insignia.
- **Time**: Observed at 0630 hours.
- **Equipment**: Equipped with small arms and two light machine guns.

This detailed SALUTE report allows the command to assess the threat and plan an appropriate response, such as avoiding the area or planning an attack with superior forces.

Example 2: Field Sketch Integration

A Ranger team on an advance-to-contact mission uses field sketches to report on key discoveries. After viewing an enemy artillery position, the team leader draws the layout, including the location of artillery pieces, supply routes, and defensive perimeters. The sketch includes:
- Key terrain features that could affect movement and tactics.
- Accurate distances between major elements to aid in artillery or air support planning.
- Enemy patrol routes that were observed, providing opportunities for ambushes.

These sketches are then used in the planning tent to fine-tune the approach and ensure all units are aware of the threats and key advantages in the terrain.

Example 3: Captured Material and POW Handling

During a night operation, Ranger soldiers capture an enemy station, seizing papers and taking numerous detainees. The documents, which include maps and communication records, are instantly tagged with the time and location of capture and returned to intelligence officials for prompt study. The prisoners are quickly and humanely segregated and searched under the 5-S protocol:
- **Search**: Thoroughly searched to ensure no weapons or intelligence material is concealed.
- **Silence**: Prevented from communicating with each other to avoid collusion.
- **Segregate**: Separated based on rank and role to facilitate more effective interrogation.
- **Safeguard**: Protected under the rules of the Geneva Convention to maintain ethical standards.
- **Speed to the Rear**: Quickly moved to a secure location for further interrogation by specialist personnel.

Example 4: Post-Mission Debriefing

Following a complex raid in urban terrain, the entire Ranger unit undergoes a structured debriefing. To guarantee uniformity, each member gives details from their own perspective, using defined reporting formats. Key outcomes from the debrief include:
- Adjustments to standard operating procedures based on unexpected enemy tactics observed during the raid.
- Identification of a new enemy communication method captured in documents, which will require signals intelligence analysis.
- Recommendations for future operations in similar environments, emphasizing the need for additional sniper cover and counter-sniper tactics.

These examples demonstrate how the methodical collection and analysis of battle intelligence directly influences tactical decisions and strategic planning inside Ranger operations. These practices not only improve the unit's effectiveness, but also help to achieve the overall goals of safety and mission success.

DEVELOPING OPERATIONAL PLANS

In the area of military operations, particularly within the specialized setting of the Rangers, the development and execution of operational plans are critical to mission accomplishment. This fundamental feature entails a rigorous approach to planning that guarantees that all aspects of the mission are thoroughly addressed and understood by all members.

The operational plan, which is typically structured as an Operation Order (OPORD), is a critical order that a leader provides to their subordinates. This ensures that certain procedures are executed with clarity and precision. The OPORD is structured in a conventional five-paragraph format, which improves the completeness and clarity of the mission directives. This format includes:

- **Situation**: Outlines the operational environment, which includes friendly and hostile forces, geography, and meteorological conditions. This part provides context and situational awareness, which are critical for the future planning and execution phases.
- **Mission**: Clearly defines the 'who, what, when, where, and why' of the operation, succinctly stating the unit's task and purpose within the larger mission framework.
- **Execution**: Details the commander's intent as well as the operational concept. This section divides the operational method into manageable tasks, defining the roles of each unit and the desired end state. This section of the OPORD also addresses the scheme of maneuver, the fire support strategy, and other critical aspects of the tactical action.
- **Sustainment**: Covers all logistical aspects of mission support, including resupply and medical plans, as well as people and equipment management. This ensures that the unit remains operationally ready and effective throughout the mission's duration.
- **Command and Signal**: Specifies the command structure and communications plan, which are vital for maintaining command and control throughout the operation.

Rangers follow this systematic strategy to guarantee that each operation is prepared with meticulous precision and strategic insight. The procedure enables a complete examination of the operating environment as well as the efficient integration of all relevant resources and information. This precise planning is critical, especially in activities where timing, precision, and adaptability are essential to mission accomplishment.

In addition to the OPORD's static components, dynamic aspects such as real-time intelligence, enemy movements, and unforeseen operational problems necessitate Rangers' adaptability and responsiveness. The capacity to modify and revise plans in response to changing situations on the ground demonstrates the skill and preparedness that characterize Ranger missions.

Rangers ensure that they are prepared to carry out difficult operations with confidence and precision by receiving intensive training in these planning processes and frequently updating standard operating procedures (SOPs). This preparation includes not only the leaders who create and disseminate operational plans, but also all soldiers who must comprehend and efficiently execute their roles within these plans.

This theoretical basis lays the groundwork for the practical implementation of these ideas, which will be exemplified in the examples below. These scenarios will demonstrate how operational plans are implemented in real-world circumstances, demonstrating Ranger units' adaptability and experience in dealing with both planned and unexpected problems during missions.

Example 1: Urban Assault Operation

Scenario: A Ranger platoon is tasked with seizing a high-value target located in an urban environment. The mission is to capture a key insurgent leader within a heavily fortified compound at the heart of a hostile city.

Mission Execution:

- **Situation**: The region of operations is characterized by thick urban terrain and a strong civilian population, which could provide cover and concealment for hostile troops. According to recent intelligence, the rebel leader is guarded by many armed troops, and there may be IED traps around the property.
- **Mission**: At 0400 hours, the platoon will conduct a raid to capture the insurgent leader located at grid reference GA123456, to disrupt enemy operations and gather critical intelligence.
- **Execution**: The operation will begin with a covert insertion two blocks away from the target compound to avoid discovery. The Alpha team will attack the compound's eastern entrance, while the Bravo team will provide cover from a properly placed overwatch position. The primary goal will be to quickly penetrate the compound, secure the target and exfiltrate before hostile reinforcements arrive.
- **Sustainment**: Logistics will include pre-staged medical support and quick reaction forces on standby. Extraction vehicles will be staged nearby, with routes clearly marked for egress under pressure.
- **Command and Signal**: Command posts will be established at a forward rally point with secure radio frequencies kept open for real-time updates. Visual signals will be used for coordination in environments where communication might be compromised.

Outcome: The precision of the platoon's movements and the clarity of the operational plan facilitate a swift and decisive operation, leading to the successful capture of the target and minimal civilian disruption.

Example 2: Jungle Warfare Patrol
Scenario: A Ranger squad is deployed to perform a reconnaissance mission in a dense jungle environment where hostile forces are known to operate small bases.

Mission Execution:

- **Situation**: The operational area is a dense jungle with limited visibility and challenging terrain. Intelligence indicates sporadic enemy patrols and a small base within the patrol area capable of housing up to 30 enemy combatants.
- **Mission**: Conduct a reconnaissance patrol to confirm the presence of the enemy base at grid GA234567, gather intelligence on enemy strength, and assess the feasibility of a follow-on direct action mission.
- **Execution**: The squad will move covertly, using natural cover to approach the suspected enemy location. Teams will rotate point duties to manage fatigue and maintain sharpness. Upon reaching an observation point, teams will set up concealed surveillance to monitor enemy movements and report findings.
- **Sustainment**: Resupply points will be predetermined, and each Ranger will carry additional rations and water due to the extended nature of the patrol. Medical evacuation points and procedures will be clearly briefed to all members.
- **Command and Signal**: Commands will be primarily non-verbal, using hand signals to maintain noise discipline. Emergency frequencies will be established, with periodic check-ins to the base to update on the patrol status.

Outcome: The thorough reconnaissance yields significant insights into adversary actions, which aids strategic planning for future operations against hostile forces in the vicinity. The patrol is carefully planned and executed to minimize exposure to enemy forces and environmental dangers.

These examples illustrate how the theoretical principles of operational planning are applied in concrete scenarios, demonstrating the adaptability, precision, and effectiveness of Ranger training and execution in diverse operational contexts.

ADAPTIVE TACTICAL ADJUSTMENTS

In modern military operations, particularly those involving elite forces such as Rangers, tactical adaptability is just as important as the initial strategy. Adaptive tactical adjustments are changes made during an operation in response to new information, unexpected enemy activities, or developments in the operational environment. This adaptable method assures operational success by allowing units to react quickly to challenges and opportunities.

Principles of Adaptive Tactical Adjustments:

1. **Dynamic Decision Making**: Commanders must be able to make quick, informed judgments using real-time battlefield information.
2. **Flexibility**: Units must be prepared to switch from one tactic to another, adapting their methods according to the situation without hesitation.
3. **Situational Awareness**: Continuous monitoring of the operational environment is essential to anticipate changes and react appropriately.
4. **Communication**: Effective communication channels must be maintained at all levels to ensure that changes in tactics are clearly understood and implemented promptly.
5. **Rehearsals and Drills**: Regular training in multiple scenarios enables units to execute complex adjustments smoothly under stress.

These principles guide the development of operational plans that are not rigid but are flexible frameworks within which units can maneuver as situations evolve on the ground.

Example 1: Urban Raid Adjustment

Scenario: A Ranger team is tasked with capturing a high-value target in an urban setting. Initial intelligence suggested the target would be in a specified safe house.

Adjustment: During the operation, real-time UAV surveillance reveals the target has moved to a nearby location, heavily fortified and guarded.

Adaptive Action:

- **Immediate Reassessment**: The commander quickly gathers the team to update the operational plan using portable digital devices.
- **New Insertion Plan**: Instead of a frontal assault on the safe house, two sniper teams are positioned for overwatch while the main team approaches the new location from a less guarded back alley.
- **Communication**: Updates are silently communicated through secure earpieces, with changes in routes and targets highlighted on shared digital maps.
- **Execution**: The team adapts their entry strategy, uses suppressed weapons to reduce noise, and successfully captures the target with minimal collateral damage.

Example 2: Jungle Patrol Ambush

Scenario: A Ranger patrol is navigating through dense jungle terrain to conduct surveillance on a known enemy trail.

Adjustment: An unexpected encounter with a hostile patrol requires immediate action to avoid detection and potential engagement.

Adaptive Action:

- **Immediate Concealment**: The squad uses the dense foliage to blend into the environment, avoiding initial detection.

- **Silent Communication**: Hand signals are used to direct movement, maintaining silence as the enemy patrol passes by.
- **Counter-Surveillance**: Once the enemy has passed, the squad leader decides to follow the enemy at a safe distance to gather intelligence on their base location.
- **Long-term Observation**: Instead of returning to base, the squad sets up a covert observation post to monitor enemy movements, adjusting their extraction timeline and informing HQ through encrypted satellite messages.

These examples show how adaptive tactical adjustments are critical to preserving the efficacy and safety of military operations, especially in dynamic and unexpected combat situations. Each choice and adjustment takes into account the overall mission objectives, the team's safety, and the potential impact on broader strategic goals.

DETAILED SUPPLEMENTARY INFORMATION

In military operations, especially those involving specialized forces such as Rangers, precise supplementary information is an important component that supplements the basic operational plans. This chapter discusses the necessity of extensive checklists and coordination mechanisms to guarantee that no component of the mission is ignored, hence increasing the likelihood of success and reducing operational risks.

Key Aspects of Detailed Supplementary Information:
1. **Precision and Detail**: Information must be specific, clear, and thoroughly outlined to avoid any ambiguities that could compromise the mission.
2. **Relevance**: All supplementary details provided must be directly relevant to the tasks at hand, providing actionable and timely intelligence that enhances operational effectiveness.
3. **Accessibility**: Information should be organized in a manner that is easy to access and use under field conditions, often formatted in checklists or quick-reference tables.
4. **Dynamic Updating**: As situations evolve, so too must the supplementary information, requiring updates in real-time to remain relevant as operational conditions change.
5. **Integration with Main Plans**: While supplementary, this information must seamlessly integrate with the main operational plans, supporting and enhancing the primary strategies and tactics.

Example 1: Coordination in Urban Assault

Scenario: A Ranger squad is tasked with clearing a series of buildings in an urban environment where hostile forces are intermixed with civilians.

Supplementary Details Provided:

- **Intelligence Checklist**: Includes recent satellite imagery of the area, highlighting new constructions and possible enemy hideouts not shown on standard maps.
- **Operations Coordination**: Details include specific civilian presence patterns and possible insurgent disguises, updates on local friendly forces, and changes in ROE (Rules of Engagement) specific to urban settings.
- **Fire Support Coordination**: Outlines designated no-fire zones to prevent civilian casualties, with pre-arranged signals for escalating or de-escalating fire support based on squad leaders' real-time assessments.

Example 2: Jungle Patrol

Scenario: A platoon is conducting a long-duration reconnaissance mission in a dense jungle environment, requiring detailed sustainment planning.

Supplementary Details Provided:

- **Logistics Checklist**: Covers water purification needs, anti-venom supplies, and specific rations suitable for humid conditions, along with detailed points for resupply based on movement predictions.
- **Movement Coordination**: Includes updates on recent enemy patrols and detailed descriptions of natural obstacles like rivers and swamps with coordinates for the safest crossing points.
- **Health System Support**: Lists jungle-specific diseases and corresponding preventative medicines, detailed evacuation plans for injuries expected in such environments, and locations for emergency medical drops.

STRATEGY AND TERRAIN ANALYSIS

In tactical operations, particularly for units like the Rangers, careful terrain analysis and strategic utilization of environmental elements are critical. Understanding and utilizing the terrain efficiently can greatly improve operating success and safety. This chapter delves into the core ideas of terrain analysis and the strategic consequences of geographic features in military operations.

Terrain analysis is an important first stage in the planning process for any military action. It entails a thorough assessment of geographical features to determine their influence on task execution. This analysis is critical for understanding how a unit might exploit terrain to its advantage, both in terms of movement and engagement methods.

Key Elements of Terrain Analysis:

1. **Observation and Fields of Fire**: Assessing visibility and the range over which actions can be effectively observed or engaged is crucial. High ground often offers superior observation and fields of fire, making it a strategic priority in many operations.

2. **Cover and Concealment**: Areas that give protection from hostile fire (cover) and enemy observation (concealment) are located in order to improve the force's survival. Vegetation, topography undulations, and urban structures can all offer valuable shelter and concealment.

3. **Obstacles**: Natural and man-made obstacles can influence the speed and movement of forces. Rivers, mountains, urban ruins, and fortified positions can act as barriers that need to be breached or circumvented.

4. **Key Terrain**: Specific locations or features that offer a marked tactical advantage to whoever controls them are identified as key terrain. Holding or controlling these areas can be pivotal to mission success.

5. **Avenues of Approach**: Identifying all possible approaches for both friendly and enemy forces allows commanders to plan movements and anticipate enemy actions. This includes assessing the ease of movement and the vulnerability of different routes.

Practical Application: Constructing a Terrain Model

Creating a comprehensive terrain model is essential for efficiently communicating terrain-related information and operational plans. This model represents the operational region in three dimensions, making it a useful visual assistance for briefing and planning.

Construction Techniques:

- **Base Material**: Use lightweight, malleable materials like cardboard or cloth as the base of the model to allow for easy transport and modification. Always include North seeking arrow and Scale on the model.

- **Topography**: Mold terrain features using clay, sand, or crumpled paper to provide a tactile sense of elevation changes and terrain texture.

- **Vegetation**: Represent trees and underbrush with materials such as moss or small twigs to add realism and help in planning cover and concealment.

- **Water Features**: Use materials like cellophane or painted surfaces to simulate rivers, lakes, and wetlands.

- **Structural Features**: Create buildings, walls, and other man-made structures with small blocks, wood pieces, or pre-formed plastic elements to visualize urban or fortified areas.

- **Markings**: Different colored strings or wires can be used to denote boundaries, phase lines, and routes. Using standardized symbols or colors for friendly and enemy forces helps in distinguishing between the two during briefings.

Every aspect of the terrain model should be designed to improve understanding of how the terrain affects operating strategies. Leaders can better strategize movements, anticipate enemy activities, and explain complex plans by visualizing the battlefield.

CHAPTER 3: TACTICAL MOVEMENTS

SAFE MOVEMENT FORMATIONS AND TECHNIQUES

In the complex theater of modern combat, the efficacy of a unit's movement formations is critical to operational success and survival. This section describes the strategic application of movement formations designed to meet the dynamic needs of combat situations, with a focus on how these formations improve control, flexibility, and security during operations.

Movement formations are the formal manner in which teams, squads, and platoons organize themselves during exercises. A variety of factors influence formation selection, including mission objectives, opponent threats, geography, and the necessity for speed and security. The primary purpose is to maximize the unit's effectiveness in confronting the adversary while reducing exposure to hazards.

Key Formations Explained:
1. **(Orizzontal) Line Formation**: This formation is utilized when maximum firepower needs to be delivered forward. All elements are aligned side by side. This is ideal for assaulting through less obstructed terrain but offers minimal protection from the flanks.
2. **Vee Formation**: This configuration, which is commonly deployed in open terrain, allows for concentrated frontal fire and a flexible response to contact from any direction. To allow for direct control over the formation, the unit commander normally leads the middle of the Vee.
3. **Echelon Formation**: Applied when there is a need to protect one flank more heavily. Units stagger themselves diagonally either left or right, allowing for strong defensive focus and offensive potential on the protected flank.
4. **Wedge Formation**: A versatile formation that provides good balance between offensive power and all-around defense, making it ideal for movement across varied terrain types. The point man leads, followed by the rest of the unit arranged in a widening formation behind.
5. **Diamond Formation**: Used when security in all directions is paramount, such as in urban or dense environments. This formation allows the unit to engage threats from all sides with equal proficiency.
6. **(Vertical) File Formation**: Most effective in confined or heavily vegetated areas where movement is restricted. This formation minimizes the unit's footprint but is vulnerable to flanking attacks.

Leaders place themselves within formations based on their capacity to command and retain control. In most cases, the unit leader is in a position to observe and guide the main effort while also quickly adapting to changing tactical   situations.
Rangers must be able to switch formations dependent on the situation at hand. Smooth transitions between formations can greatly improve a unit's tactical response and overall fighting efficiency. Leaders must constantly examine the environment, opponent movements, and the unit's condition to establish the best formation.

Advantages of Proper Formation Usage:
- **Enhanced Control**: Leaders can more effectively manage their units, maintain discipline, and communicate orders.
- **Improved Security**: Each formation is designed to maximize the unit's defensive potential while allowing for aggressive actions when necessary.
- **Optimal Use of Terrain**: Formations are chosen to exploit the natural advantages of the terrain, enhancing concealment and cover while minimizing movement hindrances.

Following the overview of movement formations, this part concentrates on the specific procedures used during tactical moves, which are critical for the unit's efficacy and security under a variety of operating scenarios. These strategies take into account the potential of enemy contact as well as the necessity for speed, control, and dispersal.

Movement Techniques Overview

Tactical movement techniques are categorized based on the level of enemy contact expected and the operational tempo required:

1. **Traveling**: Employed when contact with the enemy is unlikely. This technique prioritizes speed and control with minimal intervals between individuals, allowing for rapid movement across terrain.
2. **Traveling Overwatch**: Used when interaction is likely but not imminent. It strikes a compromise between speed and security, with longer intervals allowing for effective response and flexibility in the event of unexpected collision. The leading element pushes forward, while the main body is ready to respond rapidly if needed. To improve reaction capability, soldiers and teams are separated by greater distances than when traveling.
3. **Bounding Overwatch**: Adopted when contact with the enemy is expected or when moving through extremely hazardous regions. This strategy maximizes security by alternating movement between bounding pieces that leapfrog each other, ensuring that one element is always in position to cover the other's progress. The bounding Overwatch combines the unit into two elements: overwatching and bounding. The overwatching group is in position to fire on the advancing bounding element if needed. This strategy is organized into sequential bounds, in which each element alternates moving forward, or alternating bounds, in which the overwatch travels past the bounding element to establish a new overwatch location.

Implementing Movement Techniques:

- **Preparation and Planning**: Before movement, leaders plan routes, assign specific roles within the movement techniques, and conduct rehearsals to ensure every member understands their role in the technique to be employed.
- **Control Measures**: Leaders utilize visual signals, prearranged codes, and occasional radio communications to command and control movement, adjusting the technique as the situation develops.
- **Security Measures**: Continuous 360-degree security is maintained during all movements, with particular attention paid during halts. Teams establish quick defensive positions even during short stops to maintain readiness.

Adapting to Environmental Conditions:

- **Limited Visibility**: In night operations or other conditions of reduced visibility, the unit may modify techniques to ensure control and security. For instance, decreasing the interval between individuals or using additional visual or IR signals to maintain cohesion without compromising stealth.
- **Difficult Terrain**: In rugged or urban terrain, units might adapt by shortening bounds in bounding overwatch or using more static overwatch positions to control critical areas as the unit moves.

Understanding and using these mobility strategies enables Ranger units to move tactically and safely across the battlefield. Leaders must constantly assess the situation and make quick judgments to switch between tactics as the mission environment changes. This dynamic application of tactical mobility fundamentals promotes operational success while maximizing unit safety in dangerous environments.

MANAGING HAZARDOUS TERRAINS

Navigating dangerous terrains is an essential ability for Rangers, requiring careful preparation and execution to reduce risks while retaining operational effectiveness. This chapter describes the principles, fundamentals, and procedures for successfully managing and navigating danger zones, which are characterized as places where units are vulnerable to enemy observation or fire. The major goal when navigating any dangerous terrain is to keep the opponent from surprising or engaging the unit effectively. The procedure is carefully designed to ensure that all individuals and equipment move quickly and securely through sensitive areas without jeopardizing the objective. Key actions include:

1. **Initial Observation**: The designated team leader assesses the danger area and communicates findings to the squad leader (SL), deciding on the best course of action for crossing.
2. **Establishing Overwatch**: Before the crossing, one element (Team Bravo) positions itself to oversee the area, providing coverage as Team Alpha crosses.
3. **Controlled Movement**: The squad leader, along with essential personnel like the radiotelephone operator (RTO), crosses under the protection of Team Alpha's overwatch.
4. **Resumption of Movement**: After crossing, the team re-aligns and continues the mission at a normal pace, with the platoon leader ensuring all elements have safely passed the danger area.

Fundamentals of Danger Area Management
Effective management of danger areas relies on several key fundamentals:
- **Rally Points**: Establishing clear nearside and farside rally points for organization and regrouping if the unit needs to react to enemy contact.
- **Securing the Area**: Ensuring that both the nearside and potential far side of the area are secure before attempting to cross. This may involve reconnaissance or the use of drones or other observational tools.
- **Fire Support Planning**: Coordination of fire support to cover the movement, especially when dealing with larger or more hazardous areas.

Techniques for Safe Passage
Different techniques are employed based on the specific type of danger area encountered:
- **Linear Danger Areas (LDA)**: When crossing roads or similar features, squads halt and establish security before sending a small element to secure the far side. This element signals back when it is safe for the rest to cross.
- **Open Areas**: If detouring is not possible, the unit may need to cross directly, using smoke or suppressive fire to obscure their movement or deter enemy engagement.
- **Multiple Danger Areas**: In environments with multiple hazards close together, the unit may adopt a combination of techniques tailored to each specific threat, maintaining heightened security throughout.

Contingency Planning
Leaders must also plan for contingencies such as enemy contact during the crossing:
- **Immediate Action Drills**: If contact is made, the unit employs pre-rehearsed drills to quickly suppress the threat and move out of the danger zone.
- **Medical and Casualty Evacuation Plans**: Establishing protocols for quick medical response and evacuation routes for injured personnel.
- **Continuous Reconnaissance**: Even after crossing, continuous monitoring of the area is necessary to prevent enemy follow-ups or ambushes.

The capacity to successfully manage hazardous terrain demonstrates a unit's preparedness and tactical expertise. By following these standardized standards and practices, Ranger units improve their capacity to operate in a variety of circumstances, assuring mission success while minimizing hazards. Each step and action done is critical for the safe and effective passage through locations that present substantial tactical challenges.

CHAPTER 4: TACTICAL COMMUNICATIONS

HANDLING COMMUNICATION GEAR

Effective communication is crucial in military operations, allowing for the speedy, dependable, and secure transmission of information required for mission success. This chapter includes an overview of Rangers' key communication equipment and instructions for ensuring operational preparedness through good gear maintenance and troubleshooting.

Rangers are outfitted with a range of radio communication devices classified according to frequency bands: high frequency (HF), very high frequency (VHF), ultra high frequency (UHF), and tactical satellite. Each radio type is designed for specific operational needs:

- **HF Radios** are commonly employed for long-range communications that require bouncing signals off the ionosphere, ideal for global communications.
- **VHF Radios** operate in two bands (low and high) and are commonly used for ground-to-ground communications within a direct line of sight.
- **UHF Radios** are used for tactical and strategic communications that require penetrating urban infrastructure and interacting with satellite communication systems.
- **TACSAT Radios** provide global communication capabilities, essential for operations that require coordination with forces not in the immediate area.

Each radio system has its own power requirements, capabilities for data transmission, and unique physical characteristics. Understanding these elements is critical for picking the appropriate equipment for certain task requirements.

Characteristics and Functionalities

- **Data Transmission**: Modern military radios support encrypted data transmission, ensuring secure communication lines during operations.
- **Battery Requirements**: Most radios operate on rechargeable lithium-ion batteries with varying operational lifespans, requiring regular checks and replacements.
- **Scanning Capabilities**: Radios can be set to scan multiple frequencies, which is crucial for maintaining situational awareness and operational command across different communication nets.

Operational Use and Management

Handling and operating communication gear effectively requires adherence to several procedural steps:

1. **Antenna Management**: Ensure the antenna is securely attached and positioned correctly to maximize signal strength and reception. Regular inspections for damage and proper alignment are critical.
2. **Handset Setup**: Check the handset for any physical damage before attaching it to the radio. Ensure it is locked in place to avoid disconnections during operation.
3. **Frequency Management**: Load and verify frequencies according to the mission's communication plan. Use secure channels and encrypted modes to prevent interception by hostile forces.
4. **Preset Configurations**: Set radio presets based on the operational needs, adjusting power settings, volume, and frequency ranges as necessary for the environment and mission objectives.

Rangers must be able to use communication gear effectively. Proper training in equipment handling, frequency management and troubleshooting ensures that squads and platoons can communicate effectively and securely, which is critical for operational success and battlefield safety.

ESTABLISHMENT OF EFFICIENT ANTENNA SYSTEMS

Maintaining good communication systems is crucial in the harsh areas in which Rangers work. Antennas aid in the crucial role of transmitting and receiving signals. A damaged or badly configured antenna can dramatically reduce communication capability, potentially jeopardizing mission success. If an antenna is discovered to be faulty and there are no replacements available, field repairs or the installation of an emergency antenna are required.

Before modifying or fixing any antenna, particularly those attached to medium- or high-power transmitters, check that the transmitter is turned off to avoid serious harm or death from radiation exposure.

For whip antennas that have been physically damaged, such as breaking, reattach the pieces and restore the original length with a wire to match the broken segment. To retain signal integrity, make sure the connections are clean and secure, and if possible, solder them.

Field Expedient Antenna Construction
In situations where standard repair is not possible, constructing a field expedient antenna may be necessary. Use materials available within the environment:

- **Materials**: Copper or aluminum wire is ideal, but in emergencies, any conductive material may suffice. Ensure the wire is insulated where necessary to prevent shorting.
- **Supports**: Use non-conductive materials like plastic, glass, or dry wood as supports to isolate the antenna from the ground.
- **Connection and Insulation**: Ensure that all connections are safe and insulated correctly. Improvised insulators can be crafted from everyday items such as plastic bags or bottles.
- **Height**: Increasing the height improves the line of sight (LOS) and extends the range of communication.

Emergency Antenna Setup
Constructing an emergency antenna involves:

1. Selecting the Wire: Choose a wire that can withstand environmental conditions and has enough length to cover the required frequency wavelength.
2. Securing the Antenna: Use natural features like trees or fabricated supports to elevate and secure the antenna.
3. **Tuning for Best Reception**: Test and adjust the setup to find the strongest signal, ensuring that the antenna is oriented and positioned correctly for maximum efficiency.

Operational Considerations
When setting up antennas in the field, consider the following:

- **Terrain Influence**: Terrain features can impact signal propagation, requiring adjustments in antenna positioning and height to overcome obstructions.
- **Frequency Planning**: Calculate the necessary antenna length using the formula $X = 234/(\text{frequency in MHz})$, where X is the length in feet. This calculation helps determine the optimal length for a quarter-wave antenna.
- **Environmental Factors**: Weather conditions, local interference, and physical obstructions like buildings or foliage may necessitate additional adjustments to the antenna setup.

By understanding and applying these principles, Rangers can ensure robust and reliable communications in diverse operational environments, enhancing both the effectiveness and safety of their missions.

CHAPTER 5: ARTILLERY AND FIRE COORDINATION

FUNDAMENTAL TARGETING PROCEDURES

In military operations, indirect fire support improves the effectiveness and survivability of infantry forces. Indirect fire support includes capabilities for suppressing, repairing, destroying, or neutralizing opposing forces. Using fire support successfully during military operations provides a tactical advantage critical to achieving mission objectives.

Successful fire support hinges on four foundational tasks:

1. **Support Forces in Contact**: Providing immediate fire suppression to engaged units.
2. **Support the Battle Plan**: Integrating fire support to enhance the overall operational strategy.
3. **Synchronize the Fire Support System**: Ensuring all fire support assets are coordinated for maximum effect.
4. **Sustain the Fire Support System**: Maintaining continuous support through logistical and operational readiness.

The targeting process begins with the 'Decide' phase, where commanders prioritize high-payoff targets (HPTs) to significantly impact the operational outcome.

Interdiction Efforts

Interdiction seeks to prevent the enemy from using their resources effectively by:

- Limiting movement and options through strategic control of terrain.
- Disrupting command and logistical structures to reduce enemy efficiency.
- Delaying enemy advances to critical areas to disrupt operational timing.
- Diverting enemy resources and focus away from primary objectives.
- Destroying vital enemy resources to degrade their combat capabilities.

Effective fire support planning requires a detailed understanding of weapon systems and munitions:

- **Weapon Selection**: The choice of weapon systems is based on the target's nature, required effects, and mission goals. Factors such as range, firepower, and ammunition type are critical.
- **Munition Types**: Different scenarios require specific munitions; for example, high explosive (HE) for destruction, smoke for concealment, and illumination rounds for nighttime visibility.

Examples and Comparisons of Weapon Systems:
Mortars:

- *60mm Mortar*: Offers a max range of up to 3500 meters with munitions like HE and WP, suitable for small area targets.
- *81mm Mortar*: Reaches up to 5600 meters, providing a balance between range and firepower, effective for medium-range engagements.
- *120mm Mortar*: With the longest range of up to 7200 meters, suitable for engaging targets in depth with various munitions including smoke and illumination.

Field Artillery:

- *105-mm M119-series*: Effective up to 11,500 meters with capabilities to use HE, smoke, and illumination shells. Ideal for supporting infantry operations with precision.

- *155-mm M109A5/A6*: This system extends up to 30,100 meters using advanced munitions like M982 Excalibur, which provides precision strikes ideal for high-value targets.
- *Comparison*: The 155-mm artillery offers greater range and destructive capabilities compared to the 105-mm, making it better suited for strategic targeting across larger operational areas.

Each weapon system has an ideal engagement envelope determined by its range and munition type, which governs how it can be used against various targets. Effective targeting requires selecting the appropriate weapon system and munition type for the task, taking into account the tactical situation and desired impact on the enemy.

RISK MANAGEMENT

Effective risk management is critical in military operations, especially when faced with the inherent threats of friendly fire. This chapter describes the methodology and strategic considerations required for mitigating the hazards associated with the deployment of indirect fire support, assuring friendly troop safety while increasing operational effectiveness.

Understanding Risk Estimate Distances (RED)

Risk Estimate Distance (RED) is an important concept in combat operations because it distinguishes between the minimum safe distances that friendly soldiers should maintain and the impact of friendly firepower. REDs are calculated using the bursting radius of various bombs and the characteristics of their delivery mechanisms. They are quantified by a percentage indicating the likelihood of casualties, which is typically set at 0.1% at the moment of impact.

Application of RED in Combat

- *Operational Use*: REDs are only used in combat situations to determine acceptable risk levels. They allow commanders to make informed decisions about how near allied forces can be to the objective while avoiding severe fatalities.
- *Training Protocols*: During training exercises, Minimum Safe Distances (MSDs) are used instead of REDs to prevent accidents and ensure the safety of all participants.

The following provides specifics on the REDs associated with various unguided mortars and cannon artillery, underlining the importance of adhering to these guidelines to prevent friendly casualties:

60mm Mortar (M224):
- Danger Close Range: 600m
- REDs at various operational intensities (1/3 max, 2/3 max): 115m to 145m

81mm Mortar (M29, M29A1):
- Danger Close Range: 600m
- REDs: From 160m to 195m depending on firing intensity

120mm Mortar (M120, M327):
- Danger Close Range: 600m
- REDs significantly increase with size, ranging from 260m to 430m

105mm and 155mm Howitzers:
- These artillery pieces offer extended ranges and corresponding REDs, emphasizing the need for careful planning and positioning of troops. For example, the 155mm Howitzer (M109A6, M777A2) has REDs extending from 270m to 510m.

Operational Considerations for Managing REDs

1. **Casualty Criterion**: Determines the situation in which a Ranger is declared incapacitated following an attack, usually a five-minute assault requirement for a prone Ranger wearing cold apparel and a helmet.
2. **Echelonment of Fires**: Utilizing staggered layers of fire to maximize effectiveness while mitigating

risks to friendly forces.

3. **Command Decisions**: Commanders must weigh the risks and decide how close fires are allowed to fall relative to friendly forces, relying heavily on the expertise of Fire Support Officers (FSOs).

Target Overlays and Planning Tools

- **Use of Overlays**: Fire support overlays are essential for planning and execution, providing a visual representation of target locations, friendly positions, and planned fire missions.
- **TTLODAC Checklist**: Ensures comprehensive planning by covering all aspects of the targeting process — Target, Trigger, Location, Observer, Delivery system, Attack guidance, and Communications network.

Risk management in military operations is a dynamic and vital undertaking that necessitates a thorough understanding and careful planning. Military leaders can dramatically improve the safety and efficacy of their operations by successfully implementing REDs and leveraging systematic planning tools, hence reducing danger to friendly forces while attaining strategic goals.

HELICOPTER AND ATTACK AVIATION SUPPORT

Close Air Support (CAS) is an essential component of modern military operations, giving direct support to ground forces from airborne platforms. It includes the use of assault helicopters, fixed-wing aircraft, and unmanned aerial systems to deliver firepower precisely where it is most required, frequently altering the outcome of ground operations. CAS is critical to its capacity to immediately engage hostile targets with great precision, providing ground units with a tactical edge in both offensive and defensive operations.

CAS operations are divided into two categories: planned and immediate. Planned CAS missions are organized far in advance, with comprehensive preparation and integration into the overall mission strategy. These actions are routinely approved all the way up the Army chain of command to the corps level, ensuring that they are in line with broader operational objectives. Imminent CAS, on the other hand, is reactionary, meaning it is called upon by ground forces when unanticipated threats occur or when an imminent chance to strike enemy forces exists.

- **Planned CAS Requests**: Planned CAS requests are subject to a stringent coordination and approval process. These requests originate at the battalion level and are thoroughly recorded before being transmitted up the chain to corps, where they are reviewed in light of the larger strategic and tactical context of the ongoing operations. This level of planning guarantees that CAS missions are coordinated with other military operations, boosting their effectiveness while limiting the chance of fratricide or collateral damage.
- **Immediate CAS Requests**: Immediate CAS requests are critical for responding to changing battlefield conditions. These requests may be initiated by any unit in contact, although they are generally handled by the battalion's operations officer (S-3), the Fire Support Officer (FSO), and the air liaison officer. The timely processing of these requests is critical to the effectiveness of ground troops that require air support owing to sudden changes in the battle environment or unexpected enemy operations.

The roles of the battalion operations officer, FSO, and air liaison officer are pivotal in the swift execution of immediate CAS requests:

- **Battalion Operations Officer (S-3)**: Coordinates the overall operational planning and ensures that immediate CAS requests align with the unit's tactical movements and objectives.
- **Fire Support Officer (FSO)**: Provides the principal link between ground forces and available fire support assets, especially CAS. The FSO examines the situation, determines the requirement for air support, and processes the request to guarantee proper deployment of air assets.
- **Air Liaison Officer**: Enhances communication and coordination between air and ground forces. This function is critical to the precision and timeliness of air support, since it ensures that pilots have up-to-date information on the target and surrounding conditions.

The systematic approach to both planned and immediate CAS guarantees that air support is efficiently integrated, giving ground forces decisive advantages while reducing the hazards of friendly fire and civilian deaths. Through thorough preparation and coordination, CAS becomes a force multiplier, dramatically improving the capabilities of ground forces in complicated combat situations.

Effective Communication and Coordination in Close Air Support (CAS)

In current combat conditions, the precision and effectiveness of Close Air Support (CAS) can have a substantial impact on the result of ground operations. This chapter emphasizes the value of communication and collaboration between ground and air troops.

1. Essentials of Communication in CAS: Effective communication forms the backbone of successful CAS operations. It assures that air assistance is timely, accurate, and responsive to the changing needs of ground forces.

- *Communication Equipment*: The use of robust and secure communication technologies is critical. To achieve complete coverage and connectivity, equipment often comprises modern radios that can handle numerous frequency bands like as VHF, UHF, and SATCOM.
- *Frequency Use and Management*: Efficient frequency management is crucial to prevent interference and ensure the clarity of operational commands. Frequency hopping and encryption (COMSEC measures) are used to secure communications against enemy interception and jamming.
- *Security Measures*: Communications Security (COMSEC) is paramount in CAS operations. Techniques include encrypted communications systems such as VINSON and SINCGARS to protect tactical air controller communications.

2. Operational Considerations for CAS Deployment: The deployment of CAS must be meticulously planned, taking into consideration multiple operational factors that can affect the execution and effectiveness of air support.

- *Environmental and Terrain Considerations*: The physical landscape can drastically influence the effectiveness of CAS. Features such as mountains, urban settings, and dense forests may require adjustments in the tactics, techniques, and procedures of employing CAS.
- *Proximity to Friendly Forces*: The proximity of friendly troops to target locations needs a thorough risk assessment in order to avoid fratricide and assure ground unit safety. When friendly forces are within a preset distance of the target (usually 600 meters for artillery and mortars), procedures such as 'danger near' are used.
- *Use of Laser Designation and Marking Systems*: Laser designation systems improve precision aiming by enabling great accuracy in directing air-delivered munitions. Operators on the ground employ gadgets like the IZLID (Infrared Zoom Laser Illuminator Designator) to covertly mark targets during night operations.

The integration of helicopters and attack aviation in support roles has altered warfare dynamics, giving ground forces a significant advantage through precise and responsive air support. Mastering the art of communication and operational planning in CAS not only improves the effectiveness of military operations, but also considerably increases ground forces' survivability and success rate in combat situations.

PLANNING AND EXECUTING AIR ASSAULTS

Air assaults are critical capabilities in modern military operations, providing fast mobility and the capacity to attack with precision and speed. In the context of the United States Army Rangers, perfecting the planning and execution of air assaults improves operational success and maximizes the potential of rotary-wing forces.

Army attack aviation entails the deployment of armed helicopters to assist ground forces in close battle. These helicopters confront enemy forces with direct fire from machine guns, rockets, and guided missiles. The proximity of these aerial confrontations might vary greatly, needing rigorous coordination to minimize threats to friendly forces. Commanders and selected aerial observers are responsible for integrating attack aviation. Their responsibilities include mission planning, coordinating with aviation units, and providing real-time command and control during operations.

Robust communication systems and defined procedures are required for effective attack aviation operations. The Army attack aircraft call-for-fire protocol establishes a standardized approach for seeking aerial support, providing clarity and precision in a chaotic combat environment. Call-for-Fire The procedure entails identifying the observer, indicating friendly positions, specifying the target location and description, and making any appropriate statements such as airspace clearance and engagement directives.

The use of secure and dependable communication technologies such as VHF, UHF, and satellite communications (SATCOM) with frequency hopping and encryption provides continuous coordination between ground troops and aerial assets.

The planning step is critical to the success of aerial assaults. It includes several crucial components:

- **Mission Planning**: Detailed planning includes the analysis of enemy positions, terrain, available air assets, and potential risks. Planners must also consider the capabilities and limitations of different helicopter models regarding payload, range, and armament.
- **Rehearsals**: Conducting thorough rehearsals ensures that both ground and air units have a clear understanding of the mission, can synchronize their actions, and refine the operational plan based on practical insights.

The execution phase focuses on the operational deployment of helicopter assets in direct support of ground operations. Key considerations include:

- **Insertion Techniques**: Fast-roping, rappelling, or landing are utilized based on the mission requirements and threat assessment. Each technique requires specific training and preparation to ensure the safety and effectiveness of troop insertion.
- **Supporting Fire**: Rotary-wing aircraft may provide suppressing fire to secure the landing zone or cover the advance of ground troops. The coordination of these fire missions is critical to prevent fratricide and maximize the tactical advantage.

Rotary Wing CAS Capabilities

Understanding the capabilities of available rotary-wing CAS platforms allows commanders to effectively employ these assets in support of ground operations.

- **Aircraft and Armament**: Different helicopters offer various offensive capabilities, ranging from light observation helicopters armed with machine guns to advanced attack helicopters equipped with Hellfire missiles and 30-mm cannons.
- **Sensors and Targeting**: Modern helicopters are equipped with Forward-Looking Infrared (FLIR), radar, and laser target designators which enhance their effectiveness in target acquisition and engagement under diverse operational conditions.

Successful air assaults are characterized by seamless integration with ground operations. This includes the synchronization of maneuver elements, timing of assaults, and real-time intelligence sharing.

- **Joint Operational Tactics**: Ground commanders and air crews must follow a cohesive tactical plan that accounts for the battlefield's dynamic character. This integration is aided by ongoing communication and situational awareness updates.

Planning and carrying out air assaults necessitates close coordination, strong technical capabilities, and extensive training. As the battlefield evolves, so do the Army Rangers' tactics and methods. Rangers can dramatically improve their operational effectiveness and maintain a decisive advantage in difficult combat scenarios by using rotary-wing weapons' speed, firepower, and adaptability.

The Essence of Reverse Planning in Air Assaults

Successful air assaults are supported by rigorous reverse-sequence planning, which evaluates each phase of the operation from the objective to the point of departure. This approach assures that all components of the assault are coordinated and possible.

1. **Ground Tactical Plan**: This foundational plan details the actions required within the objective area to accomplish the mission and lays out subsequent maneuvers.
2. **Landing Plan**: Coordinated with the ground tactical plan, it sequences the arrival of units to ensure they are ready to execute the mission upon landing.
3. **Air Movement Plan**: Based on the first two plans, it schedules the flight paths and timings to move troops and equipment efficiently.
4. **Loading Plan**: Ensures that personnel and equipment are loaded systematically onto the correct aircraft, maintaining unit integrity and combat readiness.
5. **Staging Plan**: Organizes the movement of troops and equipment to the pickup zones, aligning with the overall timing of the air assault.

Selection and Preparation of Pickup Zones (PZs) and Landing Zones (LZs)

Careful selection of PZs and LZs is crucial for the safe and effective insertion and extraction of assault forces. Leaders must consider multiple factors:

- **Size and Surface**: Ensure the zone can accommodate the aircraft and is free from loose debris that could hinder operations.
- **Slope**: Ideal landing areas are relatively flat; excessive slopes can complicate landing and takeoff.
- **Obstacles**: Identify and mark any potential hazards that could affect the approach and departure paths.
- **Wind Conditions**: Aircraft should approach and depart into the wind to maximize control and safety.

Marking of zones varies between day and night operations, utilizing different signals like panels, lights, or chemlights to guide pilots effectively.

Air Assault Formations and Tactical Implications

Understanding the differences between various air assault formations is critical for improving air assault force deployment and operational performance. Each arrangement is intended to exploit specific tactical benefits while minimizing inherent hazards. Here's a deeper look at each:

1. Heavy Left/Right Formation

- *Description*: This formation involves aircraft aligned in a manner where the firepower is concentrated on either the left or the right side.
- *Tactical Use*: It is primarily used when the threat is expected from a specific side. The alignment allows

for concentrated suppressive fire from the heavy side towards the threat, protecting the insertion of troops.

- *Considerations*: Requires a larger landing area to ensure safe spacing between aircraft. The formation's layout can limit the suppressive fire capabilities of inboard gunners due to reduced fields of fire across the formation.

2. Diamond Formation

- *Description*: Aircraft are positioned at four points resembling a diamond shape, providing a 360-degree defensive posture.
- *Tactical Use*: Ideal for landing in hotspots where threats can come from any direction. The formation allows for an all-around defensive setup immediately upon landing.
- *Considerations*: While it offers excellent defensive coverage, the diamond formation restricts the inboard gunners' ability to provide effective suppressive fire, as their angles of fire can be obstructed by other aircraft.

3. Vee and Echelon Formations

- *Description*:
  1. Vee Formation: Aircraft are arranged in a 'V' shape, ideal for focusing firepower forward.
  2. Echelon Formation: Similar to the Vee but extended to either left or right, focusing on lateral deployment.
- *Tactical Use*: Both formations allow for quick deployment and excellent forward or side firepower. They are suitable for quick assaults where speed and immediate action are necessary upon landing.
- *Considerations*: These formations require more extensive landing areas and careful coordination to prevent overlapping fields of fire and ensure safe troop deployments.

4. Trail and Staggered Trail Formations

- *Description*:
  1. Trail Formation: Aircraft follow one another in a straight line, suitable for narrow landing zones.
  2. Staggered Trail: A variation where aircraft are aligned offset to the left and right, resembling a zigzag pattern.
- *Tactical Use*: These formations are beneficial for deployments along linear or restricted landing zones. They facilitate rapid dispersal of forces upon landing and immediate transition to combat operations.
- *Considerations*: While offering rapid deployment, these formations may limit the effectiveness of suppressive fire due to the linear nature, potentially exposing aircraft to lateral threats.

Tactical Loading and Off-loading Techniques

Efficient management of loading and off-loading is pivotal in maintaining operational tempo and ensuring unit readiness upon arrival.

1. Loading Techniques

- *Structured Approach*: Units are assigned specific aircraft ahead of time, known as "chalks," which include not only personnel but also their equipment and supplies. This ensures that each unit arrives with the necessary resources to begin operations immediately.
- *Cross-Loading*: Critical assets and command elements are distributed across different aircraft to mitigate the risk of losing entire command units or essential equipment in case an aircraft is downed.

2. Off-loading Techniques

- *Rapid Deployment*: Troops exit the aircraft swiftly and secure the perimeter to allow subsequent waves of aircraft to land safely. Speed is crucial to minimize exposure to hostile fire.
- *Sequential Off-load*: Ensures that units disembark in a pre-planned order that aligns with their operational roles on the ground, facilitating an organized transition to ground operations.

Safety Protocols and Emergency Procedures

Safety remains the highest priority, governed by strict protocols that every participating member must follow.

Approach and Departure

- **Safety Angles**: Aircraft are approached from specific angles that are deemed safest, usually from the sides, avoiding the dangerous rotor wash and tail rotor areas.
- **Communication Protocols**: Pilots and ground units maintain open lines of communication to adjust quickly to changing conditions or threats.

Weapon Handling

- **Rules of Engagement**: Soldiers are instructed on how to handle their weapons safely around aircraft, including the orientation of weapon muzzles and the conditions under which they should be loaded or unloaded.

Emergency Procedures

- **Briefings**: Regular safety briefings are conducted to ensure all personnel are familiar with emergency egress procedures and can react swiftly to any incident, from a crash landing to a fire on board.

Army Rangers and their officers can carry out sophisticated air assaults with precision and safety if they follow these thorough standards and capitalize on the tactical advantages of diverse air assault formations. This thorough planning and execution structure guarantees that forces are not only adequately prepared, but also flexible to the changing nature of modern combat operations.

CHAPTER 6: AUTOMATIC WEAPON STRATEGIES

DEPLOYMENT TECHNIQUES AND DETAILS

Machine guns are the backbone of the Ranger unit's armament, giving greater range and accuracy than individual soldiers' weapons. The M249, M240B, M2, and MK19 are each intended for a unique operational duty, ranging from small squad automatic guns to heavy support arms capable of decimating defended positions.

The M249 is a 5.56-mm light machine gun used to provide cover fire during infantry operations. It weighs roughly 16.41 pounds and has an effective range of up to 900 meters. The M240B is significantly heavier at 27.6 pounds, utilizes 7.62-mm bullets, and has a slightly longer effective range of roughly 1,100 meters for area targets.

The M2.50-caliber machine gun provides substantial firepower and has an effective range of up to 1,830 meters, making it excellent for destroying light vehicles and personnel targets. The MK19 grenade launcher completes the arsenal, capable of launching 40-mm explosive rounds up to a range of 2,212 meters, offering both suppression and explosion effects against entrenched enemy positions.

The operational characteristics of these guns differ, with the M249 and M240B capable of firing at rates of up to 850 and 950 rounds per minute, respectively. In contrast, the heavier M2 functions at a slower rate, assuring long-term firepower. These capabilities necessitate the operator's ability to efficiently manage heat and barrel wear, as well as protocols for fast barrel replacements during prolonged fire engagements.

Understanding the fundamental concepts of machine gun fire is crucial for effective employment. These concepts include:

- **Line of Sight**: The line that runs directly from the gunner's eye to the target via the sights. Maintaining a clear line of sight is critical for accuracy and effectiveness.
- **Burst of Fire**: Several bullets fired in quick succession with the same height and point of aim. Control of burst length is essential to conserve ammunition and manage barrel heat.
- **Trajectory**: The path the projectile follows from the muzzle to the target, which curves due to gravity and other environmental factors.
- **Maximum Ordinate**: The trajectory's highest point above the line of sight, which is usually around two-thirds of the way to the target.
- **Cone of Fire**: The pattern of multiple trajectories caused by slight differences in each round's path due to vibration, wind, and other factors.
- **Beaten Zone**: The circular pattern in which rounds from the cone of fire hit the surface or target. The shape and size of the beaten zone vary based on range and the angle of fire.

Machine gun teams can optimize their impact on the battlefield by effectively implementing these strategies. For example, deploying machine guns to take advantage of the battered zone can dramatically expand their area of effect, especially against enemy troop formations.

A machine gun team can achieve enfilade fire by aligning the long axis of the battered zone with the enemy's movement or defensive positions, ensuring that the maximum amount of rounds land within the target area, significantly enhancing the lethality of each burst. Ranger units may dominate the battlefield by properly understanding and using these principles, providing critical fire support while suppressing opponent movements and counterattacks.

These technical and conceptual foundations form the core of machine gun deployment in Ranger operations, emphasizing the necessity of precision, discipline, and tactical acumen in employing one of the most powerful tools in the infantry arsenal.

Strategic Deployment and Combat Scenarios

In modern combat, the strategic placement of machine guns inside a Ranger unit is critical to establishing battlefield superiority. Machine guns provide the long range, firepower, and accuracy required to suppress and defeat enemy forces before they can engage.

Machine guns such as the M249, M240B, M2, and MK19 fulfill a variety of functions, including suppressive fire and engagement of reinforced positions. The efficiency of these weapons is determined by their strategic deployment, which should take into account aspects like as line of sight, maximum effective range, and physical topography, all of which can either provide benefits or limit their operational effectiveness.

For example, in urban situations, shorter range and greater rates of fire prioritize immediate engagement capabilities, as demonstrated by the M249. In contrast, open terrains that enable for long-range engagements benefit from the M2 .50-caliber machine gun's increased range and lethality.

Machine gun deployment is meticulously planned and executed in reverse order to guarantee that all components of the operation are adequately addressed. This systematic strategy guarantees that every stage of the operation is aligned with the overall mission objectives.

1. **Ground Tactical Plan**: The foundation of the deployment plan, outlining the principal objectives and tactical movements. It discusses the importance of machine gun teams in attaining mission-specific objectives such area denial, enemy suppression, and direct engagement.
2. **Landing Plan**: Coordinates the deployment of machine gun squads to the operational area. It guarantees that troops arrive at predefined areas fully armed and prepared to engage. This plan is critical for missions that need quick deployment and swift response upon arrival.
3. **Air Movement Plan**: Details the aerial routes and timelines for transporting machine gun teams and their equipment from pickup zones (PZs) to landing zones (LZs). This plan is closely tied to the flight capabilities and availability of air assets.
4. **Loading Plan**: Ensures that machine guns, ammunition, and support equipment are loaded onto the appropriate aircraft in a manner that maintains unit integrity and operational readiness upon arrival.
5. **Staging Plan**: Outlines the sequence of events preceding the deployment, including the gathering of soldiers and equipment at the PZ. This strategy is crucial for keeping order and ensuring that all teams are properly briefed and equipped before departing on the mission.

Machine Gun Formations and Their Tactical Implications

Different air assault formations such as the heavy left/right, diamond, vee, echelon, trail, and staggered trail are employed based on the mission's tactical requirements and the terrain of the LZ:

- **Diamond Formation**: Ideal for rapid deployment with all-round security but limits inboard gunners' suppressive fire.
- **Vee Formation**: Allows rapid deployment to the front, useful in forward assault operations.
- **Echelon and Trail Formations**: Facilitate flank security and are preferred in operations requiring lateral movement across the battlefield.

Each formation has its pros and cons, affecting how machine gun teams can deploy, engage, and maneuver. The choice of formation can significantly impact the effectiveness of machine gun fire, influencing the outcome of combat engagements.

Classes of Machine Gun Fire

Understanding the classes of machine gun fire is essential for employing these weapons to their fullest tactical advantage. Each class has specific applications depending on the terrain and the nature of the target.

1. **Grazing Fire**: Achieved when the fire cone's center cannot reach a height more than one meter above the surface. This class works best on flat or uniformly sloping ground, creating a continuous

beaten zone that maximizes impact possibilities.

2. **Plunging Fire**: Occurs when the ground between the weapon and the target is uneven or when engaging targets at long ranges from higher elevations. This class is ideal for engaging targets in dead ground or on reverse slopes.

3. **Enfilade Fire**: The most ideal class is one in which the beaten zone's long axis aligns with the hostile configuration. This is particularly effective against linear or columnar targets as it maximizes the effect of each round.

4. **Flanking Fire**: Directed against the side of a target formation. While it is less effective against columns, it is ideal for engaging linear targets such as enemy trenches or defensive positions.

5. **Oblique Fire**: Involves engaging the target at an angle other than a right angle. This class is often used when the terrain or tactical situation does not permit an enfilade or flanking fire.

Each class of fire provides various tactical advantages and should be chosen based on the mission needs and battlefield conditions. When preparing fire plans, leaders must examine aspects such as hostile approach directions, terrain characteristics, and friendly force disposition.

- **Integration with Combined Arms**: Machine gun fire must be coordinated with other arms, such as artillery and mortars, to seal off enemy withdrawal routes or prevent reinforcement, maximizing the effectiveness of the combined arms approach.

- **Adaptability in Combat**: Leaders should be prepared to switch between classes of fire as the tactical situation evolves, adapting to the enemy's movements and exploiting new vulnerabilities as they arise.

Effective machine gun use is a critical component of Ranger tactical operations, capable of tipping the balance of a conflict. Ranger units can control the battlefield by carefully picking fields of fire and applying various types of machine gun fire, disrupting and destroying opponent forces before they can engage. This chapter not only provides as a tactical guidance for the use of machine guns, but it also emphasizes the strategic depth required throughout the planning and execution phases of Ranger missions.

OPERATIONAL TACTICS FOR OFFENSIVE AND DEFENSIVE SCENARIOS

Effective offensive operations in Ranger troops are mainly based on two pillars: fire and movement. This chapter delves into the deployment of machine guns in the offense, demonstrating how their coordinated use allows the maneuver elements to engage the adversary effectively while minimizing exposure to return fire. Understanding the subtleties of various types of fire and their strategic use can considerably improve the effectiveness of offensive operations.

The Essence of Fire and Movement

1. **Interdependency**: Fire and mobility are linked actions. The success of one is frequently dependent on the other, especially while under enemy fire. Without the protection of effective fire, maneuver elements would suffer unsustainable losses.
2. **Covering Fires**: These are critical for obtaining fire dominance, which enables for safe movement of infantry units. The fundamental purpose of offensive activities is to advance effectively in order to capture, occupy, and hold critical enemy sites, rather than simply delivering fire.

Classes of Fire in Offensive Operations

Understanding the application of various classes of fire is crucial in maximizing the tactical advantage on the battlefield:

1. **Fixed Fire**: Targets a stationary point with minimal adjustments once the burst has begun. This is typically used for well-defined targets where the beaten zone completely encompasses the target area.
2. **Traversing Fire**: Used against wider targets with minimal depth. Gunners adjust the fire's direction across the target's width without changing the elevation.
3. **Searching Fire**: Adjusts the fire in elevation to engage targets at varying distances along the gun's line of fire, ideal against deep formations.
4. **Traversing and Searching Fire**: A effective combination for targets with both width and depth that necessitates changes in both direction and height.
5. **Swinging Traverse and Free Gun Fire**: These are used against rapidly moving or wide targets requiring significant horizontal movements and rapid rates of fire.

Machine Gun Deployment in Offensive Operations

The base of fire element, typically comprised of medium machine guns like the M240B and M249, plays a pivotal role:

1. Tasks and Responsibilities:

- Suppress key enemy weapons.
- Prevent enemy's effective return fire.
- Fix the enemy in position and isolate by cutting off reinforcement routes.
- Adjust fire to support the assault element directly.

2. Operational Techniques:

- Establish initial heavy fire to gain superiority.
- Conserve ammunition with a sustained rate of fire.
- Intensify firing when the assault nears the objective.
- Coordinate the lift and shift of fires to avoid fratricide and continue suppression.

Support by Fire Position (SBF)
The SBF position is critical for maintaining pressure on the enemy while the assault element maneuvers. Key considerations include:
- **Positioning**: Ensuring the SBF is in a location that maximizes the effectiveness of the machine guns over the battlefield.
- **Controlled Occupation**: Stealthy movement into the SBF position, ensuring guns are ready to cover assigned sectors immediately.
- **Withdrawal from SBF**: Executed in a controlled manner to maintain covering fire as long as necessary, then withdrawing without compromising the unit's security.

Coordinating Fire and Maneuver
1. **Integration with Maneuver Elements**: Sometimes machine guns move with the assault units to provide close support, especially in complex terrain where control and direct fire support are crucial.
2. **Sector and Fire Control**: Assigning specific sectors or zones of fire for each machine gun team ensures comprehensive coverage and prevents gaps in the firing line.

The strategic deployment of machine guns in offensive operations is a complex procedure that necessitates thorough preparation and execution. Ranger troops can improve their operational effectiveness by successfully employing several types of fire and maintaining a strong base of fire, allowing for successful assaults across a wide range of combat conditions.

Defensive Tactics and Machine Gun Utilization in Ranger Operations
Defensive operations are an important part of military tactics, especially for Ranger forces, which rely heavily on machine guns. This chapter looks at how machine guns can be strategically deployed in defensive settings to ensure extensive coverage of the battlefield and effectively deter enemy advances.

Strategic Placement of Machine Guns
1. **Primary Role and Positioning**: In a defensive arrangement, machine guns' principal function is to provide a wide range and volume of fire to cover the squad's operational front. Effective location is critical, with the goal of providing accessibility, cover, and concealment to allow the guns to protect the defensive position's front, flanks, and rear.
2. **Positional Requirements**:
   - *Primary Position*: Maximizes the effectiveness in covering assigned sectors and can be rapidly adjusted to respond to enemy movements.
   - *Alternate Position*: Used when the primary position is compromised or to provide additional angles of fire.
   - *Supplementary Position*: Ensures coverage of unexpected avenues of enemy approach, enhancing the unit's defensive flexibility.

Enhancing Defensive Firepower
1. **Interlocking Fires**: Machine guns are positioned so that their fields of fire overlap with those of surrounding units. This setup ensures that any enemy advances are met with unrelenting and synchronized machine gun fire, boosting the unit's defensive lethality.
2. **Final Protective Fires**: In critical situations, machine guns deliver a continuous barrier of fire designed to halt enemy movements across defensive lines effectively.
3. **Employment of Medium Machine Guns**:

- *Range and Coverage*: Medium machine guns like the M240B are used to engage the enemy at maximum ranges, taking advantage of their long-range capabilities and accuracy.
- *Grazing and Enfilade Fires*: These firing techniques are utilized to maximize damage and disruption against enemy formations, especially in open terrain.

Tactical Considerations for Machine Gun Use

1. **Covering Obstacles and Flanks**: Machine guns cover tactical obstacles such as wire entanglements and anti-tank ditches, and also provide flanking fire to prevent enemy encirclement.
2. **Integration with Maneuver Elements**: Machine guns support counterattacks by delivering suppressive fire, aiding friendly forces as they maneuver to regain positions or repel enemy assaults.

Machine Gun Control and Coordination

1. **Control Measures**: Leaders employ various methods to control machine gun fire during the chaos of battle. These include oral commands, hand signals, prearranged signals, and direct communication.
2. **Fire Commands**:
   - *Alert and Direction*: Inform gun crews of the imminent engagement and direct their attention towards the target.
   - *Description and Range*: Provide details about the target and adjust fire settings accordingly.
   - *Method of Fire*: Specify the type of fire required—fixed, traversing, searching, or a combination, depending on the situation.
   - *Command to Open Fire*: The final command that initiates the action, ensuring all teams are synchronized in their efforts.

The strategic use of machine guns in defensive operations necessitates careful planning, strong control measures, and competent leadership. By leveraging the capabilities of these weapons, Ranger troops improve their defensive stance, making them powerful opponents capable of defending critical terrain in severe conditions. This chapter discusses not only the technical aspects of machine gun use, but also the tactical skills required to optimize their use in complex defensive circumstances.

CHAPTER 7: EXPLOSIVE HANDLING TECHNIQUES

INTRODUCTION TO DEMOLITION MATERIALS

In this chapter, we look at the important characteristics of demolition materials used in modern Ranger operations. Understanding the qualities, usage, and safety precautions associated with various explosives is critical for Rangers who are expected to operate in high-risk situations. This knowledge supports operational effectiveness and safety while maintaining mission integrity and staff well-being.

Classification and Characteristics of Explosives

- **Low Explosives**: Low explosives, like black powder, are used when a less intense, more controlled effect is desired. They typically have a detonation velocity of less than 1,300 feet per second. They are suited for situations that require pushing or heaving rather than fragmentation, such as clearing barriers or breaching in sensitive environments where minimizing collateral damage is critical.
- **High Explosives**: These explosives detonate at speeds ranging from 3,280 to 27,888 feet per second, producing significant shattering effects. High explosives, such as RDX, PETN, and TNT, are used in operations requiring massive devastation, such as eliminating heavily reinforced facilities or causing rapid combat effects like cratering for tactical benefit.

Detailed Analysis of Explosive Types Used in Ranger Operations
1. Ammonium Nitrate

- *Applications*: Widely used for bulk commercial and military demolitions, including creating access roads in construction and mining, or cratering operations in combat settings.
- *Detonation Velocity*: Approximately 2,700 feet per second.
- *Fume Toxicity*: Considered dangerous if inhaled in post-blast environments.
- *Water Resistance*: Poor, tends to absorb moisture which can desensitize it.

2. PETN (Pentaerythritol Tetranitrate)

- *Applications*: Integral component of detonation cords, primers, and booster charges. Utilized in precision demolition tasks such as bridge demolition and controlled building collapses.
- *Detonation Velocity*: 8,300 feet per second, offering high brisance and shattering effects.
- *Fume Toxicity*: Slightly dangerous; precautions needed to avoid inhalation.
- *Water Resistance*: Excellent, maintains effectiveness even in damp conditions.

3. RDX (Research Department Explosive)

- *Applications*: Used in a variety of military applications, including the manufacture of plastic explosives like C-4 and for shaped charges in anti-armor operations.
- *Detonation Velocity*: 8,350 feet per second.
- *Fume Toxicity*: Considered dangerous; proper ventilation and protective gear are required during use.
- *Water Resistance*: Excellent, suitable for use in underwater demolitions.

4. Trinitrotoluene (TNT)

- *Applications*: One of the most common military explosives, used in munitions, demolition blocks, and in combination with other explosives for synergetic effects.

- *Detonation Velocity*: 6,900 feet per second.
- *Fume Toxicity*: Dangerous, produces toxic gases upon detonation.
- *Water Resistance*: Excellent, which allows it to be used effectively in wet environments and underwater demolitions.

5. Composition C-4
- *Applications*: A plastic explosive that can be molded and cut to shape, ideal for precise demolition tasks, breaching operations, and improvised explosive device (IED) construction.
- *Detonation Velocity*: Approximately 8,040 feet per second.
- *Fume Toxicity*: Slightly dangerous with moderate fume production.
- *Water Resistance*: Excellent, retains its effectiveness even when submerged.

6. Tetryl
- *Applications*: Primarily used as a booster to initiate less sensitive explosives like TNT in military shells.
- *Detonation Velocity*: 7,100 feet per second.
- *Fume Toxicity*: Dangerous, with significant toxic fume production.
- *Water Resistance*: Good, performs well in moist conditions but not fully submersible.

7. Composition B
- *Applications*: Frequently used in military applications for its powerful explosive output, found in projectiles, bombs, and mines.
- *Detonation Velocity*: 8,100 feet per second.
- *Fume Toxicity*: Dangerous, particularly in confined spaces.
- *Water Resistance*: Excellent, ideal for amphibious operations.

8. MK19 and M2 Explosives
- *Applications*: These are typically used in military grenade launchers and heavy machine guns for suppressive fire and targeting light-armored vehicles.
- *Detonation Velocity*: For the munitions used, ranges vary but are effective for rapid area saturation.
- *Fume Toxicity*: Ranges from slightly to highly dangerous depending on the type of munition.
- *Water Resistance*: Generally good, ensuring functionality in diverse operational environments.

Knowing the qualities of these materials, such as detonation velocity, toxicity, and water resistance, provides Rangers with the information they need to select the best explosive for specific tactical conditions, assuring mission success while keeping operations safe.

Initiation Systems for Field Applications
1. Modernized Demolition Initiators (MDIs)
- *Components*: MDIs are comprised of several parts, including a variety of blasting caps, connectors, and initiation tools. These components are designed for versatility and can be adapted to a range of explosive types and configurations.
- *Functionality*: MDIs initiate a precise detonation sequence, which is essential for timed demolitions and synchronization with other operational aspects. They have options for both electronic and non-electronic triggering, allowing either remote or manual detonation depending on tactical requirements.
- *Applications*: Essential in military demolitions where precision and dependability are critical. MDIs are

utilized for bridge demolition, obstruction removal, and the secure disposal of explosive munitions. They are also used in training drills to imitate wartime circumstances safely.

- *Advantages*: MDIs provide additional safety characteristics, such as resistance to unintentional detonations produced by stray currents or radio frequency interference. The precision of MDIs enables less collateral damage and more focused explosive effects.

2. Shock Tube Systems

- *Construction*: A small-diameter plastic tube coated internally with a thin layer of energetic substance. When burned at one end, this layer sends a low-energy shock wave through the tube, reliably initiating a detonator or blasting cap at the other end.
- *Reliability*: The shock tube system is extremely dependable in a variety of environmental circumstances, including damp, windy, and electromagnetically active locations. Its design keeps the explosion wave contained within the tube, significantly lowering the chance of inadvertent detonation.
- *Safety Features*: Provides great levels of safety by isolating the operator from the explosive charge and the initial point of detonation. This isolation is crucial in activities requiring the operator to start explosives from a safe distance or in a predetermined sequence.
- *Operational Use*: Widely utilized in tactical demolitions where sequential or simultaneous explosions are necessary. Shock tubes can be easily stretched to reach several charges across long distances or in complex demolition patterns. They are especially effective in controlled demolitions of buildings and breaching operations in urban combat scenarios.
- *Compatibility*: Shock tube systems are compatible with a variety of explosive materials and can be connected to other types of initiation devices, such as electric blasting caps, to create hybrid systems tailored to specific mission requirements.

Together, Modernized Demolition Initiators and Shock Tube Systems represent advanced tools in the Ranger arsenal, enabling precise, safe, and effective use of explosives in a range of combat and non-combat scenarios. These systems not only increase the operational capabilities of Ranger units but also enhance safety protocols, minimizing risks to personnel and collateral during explosive operations.

EXPLOSIVE DETONATION AND EMERGENCY METHODS

Explosive operations in Ranger troops are distinguished by precision, efficiency, and, above all safety. Understanding and mastering the various ways of explosive detonation is critical to maintaining operational effectiveness. This chapter dives into the complex initiation systems used by modern Rangers, highlighting their importance to mission accomplishment and operator safety.

- **Modernized Demolition Initiators (MDI) Alone System**: The MDI alone system is a stand-alone solution for explosive detonation, with cutting-edge components designed for simplicity and dependability. The method starts with a secure placement of an explosive charge, such as C4 or TNT, directly on the chosen target. A distinctive marking, usually a sandbag, is placed over the blasting cap to indicate its location and offer an extra degree of safety. Connection to a transmission line, such as the M12 or M13, is optional but preferred for better control of the detonation process. The M14 cap with a time fuze is then linked to the blasting cap. The time fuze is carefully cut to the necessary delay, ensuring that the timing of the explosion satisfies tactical specifications. The charge is then primed by placing the blasting cap directly in the explosive substance. Before activation, a comprehensive visual inspection is performed to look for any signs of potential misfires, such as cracks or corrosion. The system is then activated from a safe distance with a fuze igniter, ensuring that all personnel remain beyond the blast radius.

- **MDI Plus Detonating Cord System**: The use of detonating cord into the MDI system improves the firing system's versatility and effectiveness. This system is very useful in complex demolition circumstances when numerous charges must be detonated simultaneously or in a precise order. The detonating cord is connected using "J" hooks from the M11 shock tube, ensuring strong and dependable connections. To protect the system from environmental conditions such as dampness, the ends of the detonation cord are tightly taped. This procedure not only maintains the explosive material's integrity, but also provides constant performance in a variety of operational situations.

When deploying MDIs, particularly in subterranean or quarry activities, it is recommended to use water-gel or slurry explosives to reduce the dangers associated with more volatile materials such as M1 dynamite. Under these situations, it is advisable to utilize a delay blasting cap, notably the M15, for further safety and control.

Misfires demand patience and a rigorous adherence to safety measures. A 30-minute wait time is required before any intervention is tried in misfire scenarios. Furthermore, Rangers are taught not to use too much force on shock tubes, as this could prematurely activate the blasting cap.

Expedient Explosive Devices

In dynamic combat environments, Rangers often need to adapt and create effective solutions with limited resources. These devices are crafted not just for demolition but also for achieving specific tactical objectives under varied operational scenarios.

1. Improvised Shaped Charges

Construction and Materials:

- *Design Basics*: Improvised shaped charges are made using easily available materials such as metal cones and household items like as bowls or funnels. The cone focuses the blast energy, resulting in a penetrating force capable of breaking through armor or concrete.

- *Materials*: Commonly used materials include copper, tin, or zinc for the liner, with explosive compounds like C4 molded to fit within the cone. The shape and material of the cone critically influence the directionality and force of the blast.

Application Scenarios:
- *Target Considerations*: These charges are particularly effective against hardened targets such as bunker walls or armored vehicles. The directional blast focuses energy at a point, maximizing penetration.
- *Tactical Deployment*: Due to their focused blast pattern, these charges are deployed where precision is necessary to achieve breach or disablement without widespread collateral damage.

2. Platter Charge
Design and Filling:
- *Component Assembly*: A platter charge utilizes a heavy metal plate backed by explosive material, typically C4. The charge is taped securely to ensure the explosive does not detach upon detonation.
- *Preparation and Priming*: The explosive is primed at the center rear of the plate to ensure an even distribution of force upon detonation.

Effective Use:
- *Targeting*: The platter charge is designed to convert the metal plate into a high-velocity projectile. It is best used against material targets such as light vehicles or grouped infantry at close to medium ranges.
- *Operational Considerations*: Rangers employ this device to create an impromptu but powerful breach or to clear obstacles with the kinetic impact from the platter.

3. Grapeshot Charge
Design and Filling:
- *Construction Details*: This device consists of a container filled with small metal projectiles like ball bearings or scrap metal, backed by a high explosive charge.
- *Assembly*: Explosives are packed at the bottom of a sturdy container, covered by a buffer material such as cloth or sand, with the projectiles placed last.

Deployment Strategies:
- *Engagement Techniques*: Grapeshot charges act like a large shotgun blast, effective in anti-personnel roles within a defined area. They are deployed to clear enemy personnel from trenches, behind cover, or during ambush scenarios.
- *Strategic Placement*: Ideal for defensive setups, these charges can be placed to cover fallback positions, creating lethal zones that hinder enemy movement and provide Rangers with a tactical advantage during withdrawals or counter-assaults.

The portable explosive devices discussed here give Rangers a variety of alternatives for dealing with varied tactical situations. Rangers can use these tools more effectively in the field if they grasp the ideas behind their design and implementation. These technologies demonstrate the Rangers' capacity to adapt and overcome in every situation, with invention and resourcefulness serving as vital components of their tactical arsenal.

Emergency Handling in Explosive Operations
In high-stress operational conditions, explosives must be handled precisely and safely. This chapter digs into the key features of emergency management during explosive operations, with a focus on standard operating procedures (SOPs) that increase Rangers' safety and efficiency. This chapter provides a detailed guide for managing explosive materials in a variety of tactical scenarios, covering everything from misfires and abort procedures to defining the fundamental demolition knots and setting minimum safe distances.

Addressing Misfires and Emergencies

Immediate Actions and Safety Protocols:

- **Initial Response**: The immediate response to a misfire is to secure the area and construct a safety zone. A 30-minute wait time is used to account for potential delayed detonations, during which all persons must keep a safe distance.

- **Assessment and Communication**: Following the waiting period, a bomb disposal professional analyzes the situation via remote methods, if available. Communication is critical during this phase, and it is maintained via secure channels to keep all team members up to date on the status of the operating plan and any modifications to it.

- **Abort Procedures**: If a detonation must be aborted, carefully prescribed procedures are followed. The crew in charge of dealing with the misfire will proceed with caution, making sure that all members are wearing the proper personal protective equipment (PPE), such as ballistic helmets and eye protection.

Equipment and Operational Checks:

- **Pre-mission Inspection**: Before any explosive material is deployed, it is thoroughly inspected for physical flaws such as cracks, bulges, or evidence of corrosion. These inspections serve to prevent the use of compromised materials, which could result in unintended detonations or duds.

- **Continuous Monitoring**: Throughout the operation, the condition of explosive materials and initiation devices is continuously monitored. Any irregularities are promptly reported, and corrective measures are implemented to reduce risks.

CALCULATING EXPLOSIVE CHARGES

In the field of military operations, particularly within the specific framework of Ranger actions, exact computation of explosive charges is not only a skill, but a fundamental requirement. The success of demolitions in combat or tactical scenarios is dependent on understanding the fundamental principles that govern the usage and deployment of commercial and military explosives.

Explosive charges, whether utilized for breaching, barrier removal, or gaining instant tactical advantages on the battlefield, must be calculated precisely. This requires a detailed grasp of the explosive material's properties, such as brisance (shattering effect), detonation velocity, and the physical and environmental conditions that influence its performance. Rangers frequently operate in various and fast changing contexts, thus knowing these equations ensures that they can adapt their tactics to any situation that arises.

Explosive handling and deployment require the highest level of safety. Miscalculations or procedural oversights can have disastrous repercussions, not only for the operator but for the entire unit.

Minimum Safe Distances:

Calculating minimum safe distances (MSD) is critical for protecting personnel from the effects of explosion overpressure, fragmentation, and other detonation-related hazards. MSD is influenced by the total weight of the explosive charge, the type of explosive utilized, and the surrounding conditions. For example, the MSD for open charges is drastically different from that in confined spaces or metropolitan environments, where blast effects might be enhanced by structures and hard surfaces.

Practical Examples by Explosive Weight

- *30 pounds*: For a charge weighing 30 pounds, the MSD is approximately 1000 feet. This distance provides a safety buffer that mitigates risks from the blast radius and fragmentation.
- *50 pounds*: Increasing the charge to 50 pounds, the MSD expands to about 1200 feet. This adjustment accounts for the greater explosive yield and its enhanced potential for collateral damage.
- *100 pounds*: With a 100-pound charge, the recommended MSD is about 1500 feet. This substantial distance accommodates the exponential increase in blast effects with heavier explosives.
- *150 pounds*: For charges of 150 pounds, the MSD should be approximately 1750 feet, ensuring safety against the increased range of explosive effects.
- *200 pounds*: At 200 pounds of explosive material, the MSD is set around 1900 feet, reflecting a continued scaling of safety measures in proportion to explosive weight.
- *300 pounds*: A 300-pound explosive charge necessitates an MSD of roughly 2200 feet, providing a wide safety margin to accommodate potential unpredictabilities in blast behavior.
- *500 pounds*: For a large charge of 500 pounds, the MSD is approximately 2600 feet. This distance helps ensure that the blast radius and fragmentation do not pose a risk to personnel or critical infrastructure.

For charges that exceed 500 pounds, the calculation of MSD must consider the significantly larger blast effects. The formula used is designed to scale the safety perimeter linearly with the weight of the explosive. For every additional pound of explosive over 500 pounds, add a specific number of feet to the base MSD of 2600 feet. This can be generally estimated as:

MSD (feet) = 2600 + (Total Weight of Explosive in pounds - 500) x Factor

This component is updated based on operational experience and empirical data from past demolitions to ensure that the calculation accurately matches safety criteria.

When preparing demolitions, Rangers must consider issues other than the immediate explosive impacts. Terrain, environmental factors, and the presence of noncombatants all play important roles in deciding the ultimate MSD. Detailed risk assessments and operational planning guarantee that all safety measures are context-appropriate and rigorously implemented.

Breaching Reinforced Concrete

For Rangers, breaking reinforced concrete structures is a key talent, especially in urban and fortified areas where such barriers frequently protect high-value targets. The success of breaching operations is determined not only by the amount of explosive utilized, but also by understanding the placement and strategy for maximizing the effect of the charge.

Reinforced concrete provides a substantial problem because it is strengthened to endure both environmental loads and human impacts. The thickness of the concrete and the appropriate positioning of charges have a direct impact on the success of a breaching operation.

Practical Placement Techniques

1. Initial Assessment: Before placing any charges, the thickness of the concrete must be determined. This can often be done using ultrasonic thickness gauges or by reviewing building plans when available.

2. Charge Placement: The efficiency of a charge is determined not only by the amount of explosive employed, but also where and how it is positioned. Charges for conventional reinforced concrete operations should be positioned directly against the surface to maximize direct impact and reduce energy dispersion.

- *Direct Contact*: Charges are placed in direct contact with the concrete surface, ensuring that the explosive force directly impacts the material without any loss of energy.
- *Covering Techniques*: Using materials such as sandbags around the charge can help focus the explosion's energy towards the concrete, enhancing the breaching effect.

3. Sequential Breaching: For thicker barriers, sequential breaching techniques can be used where multiple charges are detonated in a planned sequence to progressively weaken and breach the structure.

In every breaching operation, strategic considerations must drive tactical decisions. These include limiting collateral damage, protecting the safety of assault troops, and keeping operations secret. The explosive, mode of delivery, and timing of the breach must all be consistent with the overall mission objectives.

Material Factors and Breaching Charges

For Rangers, the success of breaching missions is dependent not just on the deployment of explosives, but also on a thorough grasp of the material elements that influence the explosive's effectiveness. Different materials necessitate customized ways to enable efficient and successful breaches without wasting resources or endangering personnel.

Material variables are crucial in calculating the amount and type of explosive required for successful breaching. These criteria include the target material's density, composition, and structural properties, all of which influence the explosive's contact and subsequent breaching effectiveness.

1. **Density and Hardness**: Harder and denser materials such as reinforced concrete and rock require more powerful explosives or specialized charges like shaped charges to concentrate the blast force effectively.
2. **Composition and Structure**: Materials like masonry or earth construction have varying responses to explosive forces based on their composition. For instance, masonry can shatter more easily than reinforced concrete, which may simply crack under similar conditions.
3. **Breaching Radius Considerations**: The breaching radius, or the effective range within which the explosive force will create a breach, varies significantly with material. Understanding this helps in planning

the placement and amount of explosive needed.

The application of breaching charges must be adapted to the material characteristics of the target to optimize breach effectiveness and minimize collateral damage.

- **Reinforced Concrete**: Charges may need to be larger and placed in contact with the surface to overcome the material's resistance.
- **Earthen and Timber Constructions**: These materials often require less explosive force and can sometimes be breached with less sophisticated methods, such as simple gunpowder-based charges or even mechanical tools in some scenarios.
- **Masonry and Non-Reinforced Concrete**: These materials may be effectively breached with standard charges, adjusted for thickness and structural integrity.

Calculating Explosive Needs

Calculating the necessary explosives involves understanding both the material factor (K) and the specific structural context. This calculation ensures that the charge is neither too small to achieve the breach nor too large, risking unnecessary damage and danger.

Formula Application: Use the formula $P = R^3 \times K \times C$, where P is the weight of TNT required, R is the breaching radius, K is the material factor, and C is the tampering factor. This helps to determine the precise amount of explosive needed based on the structural analysis of the target.

Finally, Rangers must be able to modify their breaching techniques to the particular properties of target materials. It enables operational success by conducting precise, efficient, and safe breaching operations under a variety of demanding scenarios. This knowledge enables Rangers to customize their actions to the realities of the operational environment, maximizing performance while reducing hazards.

CHAPTER 8: RECONNAISSANCE AND ENGAGEMENT TACTICS

COORDINATION AND EXECUTION OF PATROL OPERATIONS

In the dynamic and complex world of military operations, good coordination and execution of patrol activities are critical components of mission success. Rangers' mastery of these activities defines their strategic capabilities while also emphasizing their role as the vanguard of US Army operations.

Principles Governing Patrol Operations

1. **Planning**: The cornerstone of successful patrols is developing a simple, understandable strategy that can be quickly communicated to the smallest unit. This guarantees that all team members are on the same page, lowering the risk of confusion during important moments. Plans should be reasonable, concentrating on attainable targets and incorporating extensive rehearsals to ensure team cohesion.

2. **Reconnaissance**: Reconnaissance is an essential component of the preliminary phase since it entails acquiring critical intelligence about the terrain, enemy positions, and other tactical concerns. This principle highlights the proactive nature of patrol activities, in which understanding and anticipation are critical components.

3. **Security**: The force's integrity must be protected first and foremost. Every team member contributes to the unit's overall strength and resilience by bringing their own abilities and weapons. Effective security measures preserve combat power while minimizing vulnerabilities.

4. **Control**: Effective control mechanisms, rooted in clear operational concepts and the commander's intent, are vital. These mechanisms ensure that all available resources are judiciously managed to achieve tactical superiority at critical junctures.

5. **Common Sense**: The use of common sense, which is perhaps the most beneficial of all, is making sound decisions based on available intelligence, resources, and situation awareness. It is about adjusting to the ground realities and implementing changes that are consistent with the larger strategic objectives.

Essential Components of Patrol Operations

1. Task Organization and Initial Coordination: Initial stages involve detailed task organization and coordination, setting the stage for the operational execution. This includes defining roles, distributing resources, and establishing communication protocols.

2. Employment of Patrol Elements:

- *Reconnaissance and Surveillance Teams*: Specialized teams tasked with gathering critical intelligence and maintaining oversight on evolving tactical situations.
- *Assault Element*: Primarily focused on securing objectives through rapid, decisive action.
- Security Element: Responsible for protecting the main force from surprise enemy actions and securing key locations.
- *Support Element*: Provides necessary fire support, leveraging both direct and indirect fire capabilities to suppress enemy positions.
- *Demolition and Breach Teams*: Specialized units equipped to handle obstacles that require breaching or demolition using controlled explosives.

3. Execution and Maneuver:

- *Movement to Contact*: Detailed planning regarding the routes, timing, and tactics for approaching the objective.
- *Actions on the Objective*: Coordinated actions that involve seizing objectives, gathering intelligence, and

withdrawing before enemy forces can mount a counterattack.

- *Withdrawal and Re-entry*: Secure extraction from the operational area and safe re-entry into friendly zones.

Planning and Execution

- **Detailed Planning**: Involves the integration of intelligence and reconnaissance reports to refine the mission plan, ensuring all elements are synchronized and potential contingencies are addressed.
- **Rehearsals**: Conducted to ensure each member is familiar with their role and the actions required at each phase of the patrol.
- **Leader's Oversight**: The patrol leader maintains oversight throughout the operation, making tactical decisions and adjustments as required.

Patrol missions need a combination of strategic forethought, tactical expertise, and the capacity to adapt to changing battle scenarios. For Rangers, these operations are more than just missions; they demonstrate their talents, preparation, and dedication to attaining goals with precision and efficiency.

RECONNAISSANCE AND ASSAULT PATROL TECHNIQUES

Reconnaissance missions are an essential component of modern military strategy, providing information into the enemy's capabilities, intentions, and environment. These operations allow armed forces, particularly elite units such as the Rangers, to plan and carry out missions with a greater likelihood of success. The primary goal of reconnaissance is to collect actionable intelligence that informs command choices, allowing for precise and decisive operations in a variety of tactical contexts.

The primary objectives of reconnaissance missions include:

1. **Terrain Analysis**: Understanding the geographical layout to determine advantageous positions and identify natural obstacles.
2. **Enemy Analysis**: Gathering details about enemy positions, strengths, weaknesses, and potential intentions.
3. **Resource Identification**: Locating resources that can be utilized or denied to the enemy, such as water sources, high ground, and logistical routes.
4. **Force Protection**: Enhancing the safety of friendly forces through foreknowledge of threats and environmental hazards.

Reconnaissance Methods

Reconnaissance methods differ depending on the mission's requirements, the operational environment, and the availability of technology and personnel. Each method has various advantages and is chosen based on the need for stealth, precision, and depth of information.

1. **Passive Reconnaissance**: This strategy entails observing the enemy and the environment while concealing the presence of the reconnaissance team. Long-distance surveillance, electronic signal interception, and concealing strategies are some of the techniques used to evade detection. Passive reconnaissance is critical for maintaining operational security and acquiring intelligence without directly confronting the enemy.
2. **Active Reconnaissance**: In contrast to passive observation, active reconnaissance interacts with the environment, sometimes purposefully agitating the enemy to uncover vulnerabilities. This strategy may include patrols, manned or unmanned incursions into enemy territory, and the employment of decoys or probes to elicit hostile responses. Active reconnaissance is employed when more assertive tactics are required to gather necessary intelligence.
3. **Technical Reconnaissance**: Technical reconnaissance collects data using drones, satellites, and sensors, taking advantage of cutting-edge technology. These gadgets give real-time intelligence and can cover large areas without the risk of deploying troops. Drones, for example, may provide live video feeds, intercept conversations, and carry out radar surveillance, providing a huge tactical edge.
4. **Human Reconnaissance**: Despite technological advancements, human reconnaissance remains vital. Human workers grasp context, difficulty, and complexities in ways that machines cannot. They can enter enemy lines, engage with locals, and carry out covert missions that require human intervention. Human reconnaissance is frequently used to obtain nuanced, contextual intelligence that technological tools may miss.

Planning Assault Operations

Assault operations are the foundation of offensive military engagements, particularly among elite troops like the Rangers. These operations are distinguished by quick, decisive actions that aim to overrun, capture, or destroy opposing locations. To attain tactical superiority, rigorous planning and execution are required, with a focus on speed, surprise, and overwhelming force.

1. **Objective Identification**: Clearly define the tactical objectives of the assault. Objectives may range from seizing a strategic location to neutralizing a high-value target.
2. **Force Allocation**: Determine the composition of the assault force, ensuring a mix of capabilities such as marksmen, breachers and support personnel to address various contingencies.
3. **Timing and Synchronization**: The assault should be timed to take advantage of adversary vulnerabilities, such as during guard shifts or in conjunction with broader operational distractions. Coordination with supporting elements such as artillery or air support is critical for weakening opponent fortifications prior to the assault.
4. **Rehearsals**: Conduct full-scale rehearsals when possible, simulating the assault under various conditions to ensure every Ranger knows their role and can adapt to changes during the actual operation.

During execution, command and control must be fluid but disciplined. The assault begins with a suppression phase, which employs overwhelming firepower to reduce enemy combat effectiveness. This phase quickly transitions into the breach and assault, in which specialist teams break through or circumvent enemy fortifications while the main assault force exploits the breach. This high pace must be maintained to prevent the opposition from putting together an effective defense.

Ambush: Striking with Surprise

Ambushes are a vital technique in the Ranger tactical playbook, meant to strike the enemy when they are most vulnerable – while moving along a route or following a known routine. An ambush's success is determined by its meticulous planning and execution in complete secrecy.

Types of Ambushes
1. **Hasty Ambush**: Conducted when contact with the enemy is unexpected, and immediate action is needed. Rangers must be adept at quickly setting up an ambush without the benefit of detailed planning.
2. **Deliberate Ambush**: This type of ambush is planned based on intelligence and reconnaissance. It involves detailed preparation and the strategic placement of forces along the enemy's expected route of advance.

Planning and Executing an Ambush
- **Site Selection**: Choose a location that forces the enemy into a confined area where their ability to maneuver and return fire is limited.
- **Forces Disposition**: Arrange assault and support elements so that the enemy is caught in enfilading fire, maximizing damage and disorientation.
- **Withdrawal Strategy**: Plan a clear exit strategy for the ambushing force to disengage and move to a safe location post-engagement.

The success of an ambush is dependent on the element of surprise. Rangers must learn the art of concealment, move quietly, and communicate with extreme secrecy. Timing the ambush is critical; the opponent should be engaged when they are in their most vulnerable position within the kill zone.

Planning Raid Operations

Raid operations, a defining feature of Ranger tactics, involve focused, fast-paced strikes on specific objectives in order to capture, destroy, or disrupt enemy activities. Raids, as opposed to larger assault missions, are distinguished by their surgical nature and quick finish, with many taking place deep into enemy territory.
1. **Objective Analysis**: Clearly identify the raid's purpose, whether it's capturing high-value targets,

acquiring intelligence, or destroying critical assets. Each objective demands unique preparations and resources.

2. **Force Composition**: Assemble a team with a diverse set of skills tailored to the mission's demands. This includes demolition experts, snipers, and communications specialists, each selected based on the mission's specific challenges.

3. **Ingress and Egress Strategy**: Plan meticulous entry and exit routes that offer the element of surprise and the ability to quickly disengage after completing the objective. The use of multiple routes enhances the operation's security and unpredictability.

4. **Mission Rehearsal**: Conduct extensive rehearsals that as nearly resemble the operational environment as feasible. Rehearsals help identify potential problems in the raid plan and allow team members to fine-tune their roles.

Execution of Raid Operations

Effective execution requires subtlety, precision, and the capacity to adapt quickly. The first phase usually involves clandestine infiltration to approach the target without alerting the opponent. When Rangers arrive at the objective, they quickly convert to aggressive action in order to overwhelm the adversary, achieve their goals, and retire before the opponent can mobilize a concerted reaction.

Integrating Patrol Operations with Reconnaissance and Assault Tactics

Patrol operations serve as the backbone of sustained engagement, allowing Rangers to maintain a presence, gather intelligence, and project force discreetly and continuously.

1. **Reconnaissance Integration**: Patrols often begin with reconnaissance to gather critical information about the enemy's location, strength, and activities. This intelligence is vital for planning subsequent assaults or ambushes.

2. **Transitioning to Assault**: Decision-making for transitioning from reconnaissance to assault involves analyzing the gathered intelligence, assessing the team's readiness, and the tactical advantages of initiating combat.

3. **Ambush Tactics**: When a patrol identifies a lucrative target of opportunity, it may set an ambush. This requires quick, decisive action to position the team, prepare weapons systems, and coordinate the sequence of engagement.

4. **Risk Management**: Throughout the patrol, continuous risk assessment is crucial. This involves not only the threat from enemy forces but also the terrain, weather, and the physical and mental condition of the team.

Operational Safety and Risk Management

Safety is paramount in both raid and patrol operations. This includes:

- **Pre-mission Checks**: Ensuring all equipment is operational and all personnel are physically and mentally prepared.

- **Communication Protocols**: Maintaining robust communication links within the team and with command structures to ensure support and extraction if needed.

- **Emergency Contingency Plans**: Having robust plans in place for medical emergencies, extraction under fire, and other unforeseen circumstances.

To summarize, the effectiveness of Ranger raids and patrols is dependent on thorough preparation, disciplined execution, and the continuous integration of fresh intelligence and tactical improvements. These actions necessitate the Rangers' signature precision and professionalism, reflecting their standing as a leading light infantry force capable of carrying out complicated, high-risk operations with accuracy and competence.

PLANNING AND EXECUTING MOUNTED OPERATIONS

Mounted patrol missions are an important part of modern military strategy, particularly for troops such as the Rangers, which demand swift mobility and flexibility on the battlefield. These operations use vehicles' mobility to carry out a wide range of duties, from surveillance and security to direct combat engagements.

Mounted operations involve unique problems and benefits that must be recognized for successful performance. The most major problem is the vehicles' visible and aural signature on the battlefield. This visibility makes the unit a more obvious target, necessitating rigorous risk management. Vehicles are limited by the necessity for navigable terrain, which can reduce operational flexibility and routes. These disadvantages are mitigated by the speed and protection that vehicles give, allowing for rapid movement across the battlefield and the ability to engage enemy forces with increased firepower.

Vehicles can also move heavier equipment and supplies, enabling longer operations and better force projection. The inherent protection of armored vehicles helps shield Rangers from small weapons fire and shrapnel, allowing them to operate in difficult locations more effectively.

The successful implementation of mounted patrols is dependent on the proper application of five fundamental principles, each customized to the specific dynamics of vehicle operations.

1. **Planning**: Effective mounted operations begin with thorough planning that considers all aspects of the objective. The planning step must take into account vehicle kinds, capacities, and the characteristics of the terrain over which the operation will take place. Detailed route design, including primary and alternate routes, must take into account road conditions, potential bottlenecks, and enemy threats like ambush positions or IEDs.

2. **Reconnaissance**: Prior to any maneuver, extensive reconnaissance is required to collect as much information as possible about the operational environment. This includes comprehending the topography, recognizing enemy positions, and determining the appropriateness of routes for vehicle movement. Aerial reconnaissance and satellite images can provide significant insights that dismounted patrols may not have access to.

3. **Security**: Security in mounted operations is more than just force protection. It include securing routes, establishing quick reaction forces, and preparing backup positions. Vehicles must be outfitted with both passive and active defense systems to detect and respond to threats, as well as protocols for speedy escape or regrouping if contact is established with the enemy.

4. **Control**: Maintaining control of a fast-moving mounted patrol necessitates reliable communication systems and disciplined leadership. The utilization of modern communication technologies allows for real-time updates and alterations to the mission as it occurs. Commanders must have a thorough awareness of the operating environment and the ability to quickly communicate directives to vehicle commanders and crews.

5. **Common Sense**: Mounted operations necessitate keen judgment and the ability to make quick decisions. Leaders must use the intelligence obtained during reconnaissance, together with a grasp of the mission objectives and unit capabilities, to make tactical decisions that adapt to changing battlefield conditions.

By incorporating these ideas into the planning and execution of mounted operations, Ranger leaders can maximize the capabilities of their vehicles while limiting the inherent hazards of operating such high-profile assets in conflict zones. The following sections will go deeper into the specific planning concerns and execution tactics that are essential for successful mounted operations.

Execution of Mounted Operations

1. Staging Plan: The staging phase is critical in establishing the framework for a successful patrol. During this period, Rangers must implement strict security standards to protect the assembling area. The region is properly demarcated with both daytime and nighttime identifying marks, allowing all elements to simply travel and consolidate their forces without confusion.

- **Security Setup**: Implement a comprehensive security plan to monitor all approaches to the staging area. Early warning systems and quick reaction forces should be in place to respond to any threats.
- **Markings and Linkup Procedures**: Use standardized visible and infrared indicators to direct units to their appropriate zones. Precise linkup procedures must be implemented to coordinate the arrival of various units, ensuring seamless integration and reducing exposure time in the staging area.

2. Loading Plan: Once the staging is securely established, the loading plan is initiated. This phase is critical for ensuring that personnel and equipment are organized efficiently for rapid deployment.

- **Task Organization**: Each Ranger and vehicle is assigned specific roles, ensuring an optimal distribution of skills and firepower. The organization should consider the tactical requirements of the mission and the individual capabilities of the Rangers.
- **Tactical Cross-Loading**: To reduce the chance of mission failure due to fatality or vehicle loss, critical equipment and personnel are dispersed among multiple vehicles. This involves cross-loading communications equipment, weapons systems, and leadership elements to ensure operational capability if a vehicle is disabled.

3. Movement Plan: The movement plan is where the patrol transitions from preparation to action. Maintaining security and effective navigation are paramount during this phase.

- **Security During Movement**: Continuous situational awareness is maintained throughout the movement. All vehicles must have overlapping sectors of fire and maintain visual contact to respond quickly to any contact.
- **Navigation and Contingency Plans**: Navigators use pre-defined routes with alternate options pre-planned. Contingency plans for potential scenarios like enemy engagements or vehicle breakdowns are rehearsed and understood by all members.

4. Unloading Plan: Upon reaching the designated dismount point, the patrol transitions from mounted to potential foot movement with a focus on maintaining tactical advantage.

- **Procedures for Dismount**: Rangers dismount using drills that minimize exposure and maintain readiness. Quick establishment of a defensive perimeter ensures security as the patrol transitions to ground operations.
- **Security Establishment**: Immediate actions are taken to secure the area, with pre-assigned sectors of responsibility activated as soon as boots hit the ground.

5. Ground Tactical Plan: The final transition from mounted to dismounted operations is contingent upon the mission's requirements. This phase involves deploying Rangers according to the ground tactical plan prepared during the staging phase.

- **Transition Operations**: Detailed plans for transitioning from vehicle support to foot mobility must be outlined, considering terrain, enemy presence, and mission objectives.
- **Execution of Ground Objectives**: Once dismounted, Rangers execute their ground mission as per the operational orders. This includes navigating to objectives, engaging targets, and performing reconnaissance or direct action tasks as required.

Command Structure within Mounted Patrols

The command structure for mounted patrols is designed to maximize operational effectiveness and communication flow. Each role within the patrol is clearly defined to prevent any ambiguity under stress.

- **Platoon Leader (PL)**: The PL is the primary decision-maker and bears overall responsibility for the mission. Positioned ideally in a central vehicle, the PL has the vantage to oversee the entire patrol and make real-time decisions.
- **Platoon Sergeant (PSG)**: The PSG, as the patrol's senior noncommissioned officer, assists the PL by overseeing logistics and manpower. The PSG often travels in the first or last vehicle to respond rapidly to logistical concerns or provide combat support as needed.
- **Vehicle Commanders**: Each vehicle in the patrol is commanded by a designated Vehicle Commander (VC), who is in charge of maneuvering their vehicle and ensuring that all personnel complete their tasks. The VC communicates directly with the PL and PSG to transfer crucial information and receive directives.

Emergency Procedures for Ambushes, IEDs, and Vehicle Breakdowns

Preparedness for potential threats such as ambushes, IEDs, or vehicle malfunctions is critical for mission success and personnel safety.

- **Ambush Response**: Training in immediate action drills to counter ambushes, involving maneuvering out of the kill zone and returning effective fire.
- **IED Threats**: Procedures for recognizing and reacting to potential IED threats include maintaining vigilance, using route clearance support, and training on identifying IED indicators.
- **Vehicle Breakdowns**: Protocols for quick recovery or repair of disabled vehicles under fire cover. If recovery is not possible, procedures for destroying sensitive equipment and safely extracting personnel must be implemented.

Reacting to Contact

Despite careful planning, encounter with enemy forces is a real possibility. When a patrol comes under enemy fire, the first priority is to escape out of the 'death zone'. The conventional practice is for the first vehicle to push through the contact zone if practicable, with subsequent vehicles providing suppressing fire.

If the patrol is unable to pass through, they do a well-practiced dismount under fire. Dismounting men swiftly form a safe perimeter to deliver effective fire against the enemy, allowing other vehicles to maneuver or retire as needed. Commanders must quickly determine whether to continue the mission, call for assistance, or withdraw based on the effectiveness of the enemy's engagement.

Support components play an important part in mounted operations. They give the essential firefighting assistance, medical help, and more resources. In the event of a casualty, designated medical Rangers (combat lifesavers or medics) provide quick battlefield treatment. Casualty evacuation protocols are predetermined, with designated vehicles or air support on standby to take injured personnel to medical facilities.

After breaking contact with the enemy, it is critical to reorganize and assess the patrol's capacity to continue the operation. This includes accounting for all troops, assessing vehicle functionality, and maintaining connection with higher headquarters to report contact and get additional instructions.

Leaders undertake after-action reviews to document the lessons learned from the engagement, which are critical for modifying future patrols and training. This continual feedback loop improves the unit's tactical capability and readiness for future operations.

CHAPTER 9: COMBAT DRILLS ESSENTIALS

RESPONDING TO FIRE

Battle drills are crucial equipment in any military unit's inventory, specifically designed to improve Rangers' efficacy in combat. These exercises consist of pre-established processes that soldiers carry out automatically when presented with well-defined circumstances. The purpose is to respond quickly and effectively, reducing the need for precise orders in the heat of battle, ensuring unit cohesiveness and precision under fire.

Battle drills are defined as standardized collective actions carried out by a platoon or smaller unit in response to direct enemy engagement. Battle exercises, as opposed to conventional operations, which may necessitate careful consideration and specific commands, are intended to be carried out immediately. They are triggered by a clear cue—such as an enemy attack or a specific command from a leader—and carried out quickly and effectively.

1. **Collective Actions Without Deliberation**: Each drill is a complex activity involving numerous team members, with each individual's part clearly defined and thoroughly practiced. This enables for a fluid, instinctual response, which is critical in unexpected or abrupt combat situations.

2. **Automatic Initiation on Cues**: Drills begin automatically when appropriate cues are detected in the combat environment. These cues could range from the presence of an enemy force to the sound of an ambush. Immediate identification of these cues is a vital talent that requires much training and experience.

3. **Role of Minimal Leader Orders**: The low communication requirements of a battle drill contribute significantly to its efficiency. Leaders offer brief, clear commands as needed, but the goal is that each Ranger understands their duty and can carry it out without step-by-step instructions. This method minimizes misunderstanding and ensures a faster operational pace.

4. **Standardized Performance Across Units**: Consistency is essential when carrying out warfare drills. Each Army unit conducts these drills in a uniform manner, ensuring that the actions taken are predictable and consistent across the whole military organization, independent of the specific unit makeup. This standardization promotes interoperability in joint operations and strengthens the force's collective capability.

During patrol operations, whether mounted or dismounted, Rangers must always be prepared to respond to sudden enemy engagements. This section details the scenario setup and specific triggers for initiating the battle drill for reacting to direct fire.

- **Scenario Setup**: The unit is in motion, conducting a routine patrol or moving to a designated objective. The environment is tense, and the threat level is high due to known enemy activity in the area.
- **Specific Cue**: When enemy forces fire directly at the unit, the drill is triggered. This contact could be caused by small arms, machine guns, or other direct-fire weapons. The unexpected beginning of enemy fire acts as a clear cue for Rangers to start the drill.

Immediate Actions

Upon enemy engagement, Rangers must react instantaneously to mitigate casualties and maintain the initiative.

1. Initial Response:

- The element in contact immediately returns fire. This reflexive fire is aimed at suppressing the enemy to gain momentary control of the situation.
- Simultaneously, all personnel seek the nearest cover, minimizing exposure to enemy fire.

2. Tactical Movement:

- Vehicles in the convoy or patrol must swiftly move out of the beaten zone, the area effectively targeted by the enemy.
- Soldiers dismount if the situation dictates and move rapidly to covered and concealed positions, enhancing their defensive posture while maintaining the ability to engage the enemy.

Engagement and Communication

Effective engagement of the enemy requires precise identification of their positions and robust communication within the unit.

1. Locating the Enemy:

- Element leaders play a crucial role in quickly identifying enemy positions. Using their heightened situational awareness, they direct their units' fire accurately and efficiently towards the enemy.
- The use of well-aimed or battlesight fire is authorized, depending on the clarity of enemy positions.

2. Communication within the Unit:

- It is vital to maintain visual and oral communication among all members of the unit during the engagement. This guarantees that each soldier and vehicle commander is informed of the situation and may change their actions as needed.
- The unit leader, often the platoon leader or the designated patrol leader, must continuously communicate with both sub-element leaders and individual soldiers to coordinate the unit's response effectively.
- Commands and status updates are relayed through established communication channels, ensuring that each member of the unit understands their role and the current tactical situation.

Role of Unit Leaders and Element Leaders in Controlling the Situation

In the heat of engagement, the clarity of command and the decisiveness of leadership are paramount. Unit leaders, including the platoon leader (PL) and element leaders, shoulder the responsibility of orchestrating a controlled, effective response to enemy fire.

1. Unit Leader Responsibilities:

- The PL oversees the entire unit's response, making critical decisions based on the dynamics of the engagement. They must ensure that all elements are coordinated and that the unit's actions align with overarching operational objectives.
- The PL is also responsible for integrating support elements, such as forward observers and crew-served weapons, effectively into the engagement. This may involve repositioning these assets to maximize their impact on the battlefield.

2. Element Leader Duties:

- Element leaders manage smaller sub-units within the platoon, directing their actions during the drill. They relay commands from the PL and ensure that soldiers are effectively employing their training in fire and maneuver tactics.
- These leaders also monitor the status of their soldiers, managing ammunition, casualties, and communication within their respective elements.

Deployment of Additional Resources

The use of specialized resources such as forward observers and crew-served weapons can significantly enhance the unit's combat effectiveness.

- **Forward Observers**: Deployed to pinpoint enemy positions and call for indirect fire support. Their expertise allows the unit to utilize artillery and air support, extending the reach and impact of the unit's response.
- **Crew-Served Weapons**: These weapons platforms provide a base of fire that can suppress and break enemy positions. Their deployment is strategic, aimed at delivering sustained fire to cover maneuver elements or to prevent enemy advance.

Assessment and Decision-Making by the Unit Leader

During the engagement, the unit leader continuously assesses the situation, making decisions on whether to continue the engagement or to execute alternative tactical maneuvers.

- *Continuation or Cessation of Engagement*: Decisions are based on the effectiveness of current efforts against the enemy, the status of unit resources, and the overall mission objectives. The leader must decide if the unit will maintain pressure, redeploy, or withdraw, depending on the tactical advantage or disadvantage.

Resolution of the Engagement

Post-engagement, the unit leader evaluates the situation and chooses the most appropriate course of action:

1. **Assault**: If the enemy is deemed vulnerable and the mission dictates, an assault may be ordered to seize and secure enemy positions.
2. **Bypass**: The unit may bypass heavily fortified positions if they do not pose a direct threat to mission objectives, preserving resources for primary objectives.
3. **Break Contact**: If the engagement is unfavorable, breaking contact to reorganize and preserve force integrity might be the most prudent decision.

Final Assessment: The unit leader assesses the enemy's position, strength, and potential vulnerabilities. This assessment helps in planning the next steps, whether to re-engage, bypass, or retreat.

Reporting to Higher Command:

- Following the engagement, the unit leader reports the outcome to higher command. This report includes details of the engagement, current unit status, and recommendations for further actions or reinforcements.
- Subsequent maneuvers are planned based on the higher command's directives and the situational needs, ensuring that the unit remains proactive and mission-focused.

This systematic approach to command and control during engagements guarantees that Rangers maintain tactical dominance and adaptability in a variety of combat settings, embodying the principles of accuracy, discipline, and strategic thinking that define their role.

TACTICS FOR ASSAULT AND AMBUSH SITUATIONS

Platoon assaults are a critical component of modern military strategy, providing a decisive means for engaging opposing forces successfully. These operations are critical for gaining control of crucial sites and breaching opposing defenses. Successful platoon attacks can significantly shift the tide of larger military conflicts, emphasizing their importance in attaining operational goals.

The fundamental purpose of a platoon attack is to quickly and efficiently destroy enemy units while securing important locations and sustaining momentum in the operational area. Objectives include:

- Establishing dominance over key terrain or strategic assets.
- Disrupting enemy command and control capabilities.
- Forcing enemy withdrawal or capitulation through decisive action.

Pre-Assault Actions

Initial Contact and Response:

Upon enemy contact, the immediate response of the platoon is crucial for setting the stage for a successful assault. Actions include:

- **Immediate Return Fire**: Upon encountering direct fire from the enemy, the element in contact must respond promptly with well-aimed fire to suppress enemy capabilities and gain fire superiority.
- **Tactical Positioning**: Both vehicle operators and dismounted soldiers perform specified maneuvers. Vehicles maneuver to avoid the enemy's effective firing range, or 'beaten zone,' while dismounted troops seek cover to reduce exposure to hostile fire.

Leadership's Immediate Actions:

The initial minutes following contact are critical and require decisive leadership to steer the platoon towards a favorable outcome.

- **Platoon Leader's Role**: The platoon leader assesses the situation rapidly, issuing commands to dismount the vehicles if necessary and directing the movement of troops to advantageous positions. The platoon leader also ensures continuous communication with higher headquarters to report contact and receive further instructions.
- **Platoon Sergeant's Responsibilities**: Acting as the pivotal link between the platoon leader's orders and the soldiers on the ground, the platoon sergeant coordinates the logistics of vehicle and troop movements, oversees the setup of initial defensive positions, and manages the distribution of resources and reinforcements.

This planned technique to launching a platoon assault guarantees that every member of the unit understands their duty and is ready to carry it out efficiently under the direction of their commanders. The future phases of the assault will be significantly reliant on the effectiveness of these early operations.

Establishing Fire Supremacy

Base of Fire Formation:

The formation of a solid base of fire is critical to achieving tactical superiority during a platoon assault. The process involves:

- **Deployment of Squads and Machine Gun Teams**: The platoon leader works with the weapons squad leader to strategically deploy machine gun units across the battlefield. These squads are entrusted with provide constant, suppressive fire to pin down the adversary and limit their ability to move.

- **Optimizing Field Positioning**: The platoon sergeant is responsible for arranging squads in formations that optimize efficiency while limiting vulnerability to opposing fire. This includes determining how to best employ natural terrain characteristics for concealment and maintaining clear lines of sight for successful firing.

Assessment of Fire Supremacy:
Achieving fire supremacy requires ongoing assessment and adjustment:
- **Criteria for Suppression**: The platoon must evaluate the volume and accuracy of their fire relative to the enemy's response. Effective suppression is indicated by a noticeable decrease in enemy fire and the ability to maneuver without significant opposition.
- **Decision-making Process**: The platoon leader decides whether to continue suppression efforts or adjust tactics based on the effectiveness of the initial fire. This may involve shifting fire to new enemy positions or intensifying fire on key targets.

Maneuvering and Flanking
Tactical Flanking:
Flanking maneuvers are essential for disrupting enemy defenses and achieving a positional advantage.
- **Strategies for Safe Flanking**: Squads execute flanking moves by concealing their approach with terrain such as hills or built-up regions. The goal is to reach a vantage point from which they may successfully engage the adversary from the side or rear, disrupting the enemy's concentration and defensive setup.
- **Using Terrain and Cover**: Movement must be planned to exploit the terrain, using elements like dense foliage, urban structures, or undulating land to approach enemy positions without significant exposure.

Coordination During Maneuver:
Effective coordination ensures the success of flanking maneuvers and the safety of the troops involved.
- **Role of Communication**: Continuous communication is vital. This includes the use of visual signals and radios to keep all elements of the platoon informed of movements and changes in the enemy's posture.
- **Integration of Indirect Fire**: As squads maneuver, the platoon leader works with the advance observer to direct indirect fire support. This could include modifying mortar or artillery bombardment to discourage enemy reinforcements or creating smoke screens that disguise the movement of friendly forces.

Steps for Assault Execution:
During the assault phase, the precise execution of tactical movements is critical for overwhelming enemy defenses.
- **Movement of Assaulting Squads**: Assaulting squads advance using a combination of bounding overwatch and fire-and-movement techniques. The movement is choreographed to maintain momentum while minimizing exposure to enemy fire.
- **Fire Adjustment**: Before the assault, the platoon leader works with machine gun teams and vehicle commanders to shift or lift fires. This is critical to preventing fratricide and ensuring that flames effectively suppress opposing positions or obscure the opponent's vision, allowing infantry squads to advance.

Use of Supporting Fires
Deployment of Support Weapons:
- **Machine Guns and Vehicle-mounted Weapons**: These assets are strategically positioned to provide

continuous fire support. Their role is to suppress enemy strongpoints and cover open areas through which the platoon must maneuver.

- **Adjustment of Indirect Fires**: The advanced observer directs mortar or artillery fire to isolate the enemy, prevent reinforcement, and give cover for advancing troops. This may involve using smoke rounds to hide the enemy's view and high-explosive rounds to disrupt opposing fortifications.

Consolidation and Reorganization
Post-Assault Consolidation:

- **Securing the Objective**: Once the enemy position has been taken, teams swiftly switch to consolidation actions. This includes erecting defensive perimeters, removing residual enemy pockets, and creating observation stations to monitor enemy activity.
- **Reorganization of Forces**: The platoon leader directs the redistribution of ammunition, medical checks, and if necessary, the reassignment of personnel to maintain the integrity of fighting units.

Continued Command and Control
Maintaining Security and Readiness:

- **Command Responsibilities**: The platoon leader, along with the squad leaders, ensures that all defensive measures are in place to repel any potential counterattack. This includes placing crew-served guns in strategic places to cover the most likely approaches, as well as integrating indirect fire plans with maneuver elements.
- **Communication with Higher Headquarters**: Continuous reporting is crucial to keep higher command informed of the situation on the ground. This includes updates on troop strength, enemy movements, and logistical needs.

Ambush Preparation and Execution in Ranger Operations
Types of Ambushes
1. Hasty Ambush:

- *Definition and Context*: A hasty ambush is employed when contact with the enemy is unexpected. Rangers must react swiftly, capitalizing on the element of surprise without the benefit of extensive preparation.
- *Execution Principles*: The emphasis is on making quick decisions and taking swift action. Rangers position themselves rapidly, using natural terrain for cover, and engage the enemy with coordinated fire whenever a suitable chance arises.

2. Deliberate Ambush:

- *Preparation*: This type of ambush is meticulously planned, with detailed intelligence and reconnaissance guiding the setup. It involves specific roles for each team member and comprehensive execution plans.
- *Execution*: Deliberate ambushes are distinguished by their precision and strategic use of terrain and timing. The goal is to maximize damage and disrupt enemy operations, with each Ranger understanding their duty and the broader mission objective.

Planning and Setting Ambush
1. Selection of Ambush Site:

- *Terrain Analysis*: The selection process involves detailed terrain analysis to identify the most advantageous locations based on natural concealment and the expected paths of enemy movement.
- *Enemy Patterns*: Understanding enemy patterns is crucial. Rangers leverage intelligence reports and past encounter data to predict enemy behavior and movement, ensuring the ambush site exploits these patterns effectively.

2. Layout Planning:

- *Personnel Deployment*: The placement of soldiers during an ambush is designed to generate interlocking fields of fire that maximize damage while reducing the enemy's risk of escape. Rangers deploy themselves to cover all possible escape routes while also providing protective cover for themselves.
- *Weapons Placement*: Heavy weapons and crew-served platforms are strategically deployed to give suppressive fire, cutting off enemy reinforcements and escape routes. Lighter, more mobile weapons are utilized to engage the opponent right in the kill zone.

Execution of Ambush in Ranger Operations
Criteria for Initiation:

- *Enemy Position and Vulnerability*: The decision to initiate an ambush is critically dependent on the enemy's position relative to the ambush site. The ideal moment is chosen based on the enemy's maximum exposure and minimum ability to respond effectively.
- *Preparation and Readiness*: Rangers ensure that all personnel are in position, weapons are aimed, and communication lines are open. The ambush begins just when the adversary has fully committed to the kill zone, increasing their vulnerability.

Signal Coordination:

- *Unified Strike*: A planned signal—either visible or electronic—is utilized to coordinate the start of the firing. This ensures that all elements engage the opponent at the same time, causing a shockwave and overwhelming opposing forces before they can react.
- *Silence and Stealth*: Prior to the ambush, strict noise discipline is maintained to preserve the element of surprise. The signal to attack is often a specific, sudden noise or a visual cue that is unmistakable but not detectable by the enemy until it is too late.

Actions During Ambush
Tactical Execution:

- *Surprise and Speed*: The success of an ambush is dependent on its execution at rapid speed and absolute precision. Rangers use the first shock of the ambush to incapacitate as many enemy units as possible before launching a counterattack.
- *Dynamic Maneuvering*: Squads maneuver within the designated ambush area to maintain the element of surprise, using the terrain and any available cover to their advantage.

Sealing Escape Routes:

- *Overlapping Fire*: Weapons are strategically placed to create overlapping fields of fire that cover all possible escape routes. This method ensures that the enemy is caught in a crossfire if they attempt to break out of the kill zone.
- *Containment Tactics*: Ranger squads are responsible with blocking escape routes, using swift mobility and shooting to cover any holes where the enemy could retreat. To prevent opponent mobility, these teams use a combination of direct fire, barricades, and natural terrain characteristics.

Post-Ambush Coordination:

- *Quick Assessment*: Immediately following the ambush, squad leaders perform a quick but thorough assessment of enemy casualties, Ranger positions, and ammunition levels.
- *Communication*: Information about the outcome of the ambush and any immediate follow-up actions are swiftly communicated to higher command, ensuring that all participating units are promptly updated on

the situation.

Withdrawal Tactics
Methods for Breaking Contact:

- *Smoke Deployment*: Rangers utilize smoke grenades or smoke shells to obscure enemy vision, creating a visual barrier that facilitates safe withdrawal.
- *Cover Utilization*: Leveraging the terrain and any available cover is critical for minimizing exposure during the withdrawal. Rangers are trained to move swiftly and silently, using the environment to shield their movements from the enemy.
- *Alternating Bounding*: Teams employ bounding techniques, where one element covers while the other moves. This alternating pattern ensures that there is always a covering fire, providing continuous protection as units pull back from the ambush site.

Post-Ambush Reorganization
Rally and Accountability:

- *Rally Points*: Units regroup at a pre-determined rally point that is secure and away from the ambush site. This location is chosen for its defensibility and ease of access for all units involved in the ambush.
- *Personnel and Equipment Checks*: Immediate accountability is taken for all personnel and equipment. This rapid muster ensures that any losses are quickly identified, and necessary actions are taken to address them.
- *Casualty Care and Resupply*: Casualties are treated with priority, and medical evacuation procedures are initiated if required. Simultaneously, units resupply and prepare for potential follow-up actions or further movements.

Assessment and Communication:

- *Effectiveness Evaluation*: Commanders assess the effectiveness of the ambush based on enemy casualties, equipment losses, and the overall disruption caused to enemy operations.
- *Higher Command Reporting*: A detailed report is sent to higher headquarters outlining the results of the ambush and the unit's current status, ensuring that the broader operational picture is updated.

Integration with Platoon Assault
Transition Strategies:

- *From Ambush to Assault*: When the situation allows, Rangers may transition from an ambush to a full-scale assault. This decision is based on the success of the ambush, the vulnerability of the enemy, and the availability of additional assault forces.
- *Coordination with Main Assault Forces*: Effective communication and pre-planned coordination are essential. The ambush element must synchronize its actions with the main assault forces to capitalize on the enemy's disarray and secure strategic advantages.

Synchronization with Mission Objectives:

- *Alignment with Broader Goals*: Every ambush is planned with an understanding of the overarching mission objectives. The decision to transition to an assault or to withdraw after an ambush is influenced by how these actions support the overall mission.
- *Platoon Leader's Decision-Making*: The platoon leader evaluates whether continuing with an assault offers strategic value or if withdrawal is prudent to preserve force strength for future operations.

This chapter describes the tactical techniques Rangers use to evacuate and reorganize following an ambush, guaranteeing operational security and preparation for future actions. It emphasizes the integration of these techniques with larger operational strategies, as well as Rangers' agility and tactical acumen in complicated combat settings.

CHAPTER 10: HIGH-ALTITUDE WARFARE PREPARATION

PLANNING AND EQUIPMENT

Mountaineering capabilities are an essential part of modern military operations, providing strategic benefits in a variety of worldwide terrains. The ability to travel and function efficiently in hilly areas increases a unit's tactical mobility and opens up channels for both assault and defense that are inaccessible to less equipped or trained personnel. Mountaineering skills enable military units, such as the Rangers, to conduct operations with a high level of stealth and surprise, which is often required in asymmetric warfare circumstances.

Mountain warfare has historically played an important role in a variety of global conflicts. From the Alps in World War I to the harsh terrains of Afghanistan in recent conflicts, the capacity to fight and maneuver in hilly places has frequently been a deciding factor. These operations have demonstrated that soldiers trained in sophisticated mountaineering methods may use the terrain to their advantage, resulting in tactical benefits that frequently outweigh the inherent challenges of these situations.

Mountain operations training is intended to prepare military troops to face the unique problems that hilly terrains present. This training focuses not only physical fitness, but also technical abilities that improve survival and combat efficiency in adverse situations. The thorough training programs are designed to establish a high degree of expertise in negotiating tough terrains, allowing soldiers to work safely and effectively.

Operational Planning for Mountain Warfare

Mountain warfare necessitates a different approach to operations planning due to the terrain's inherent tactical difficulties. Commanders must consider how the topography affects mobility, lines of sight, and communications when developing their strategy. This necessitates rigorous planning and the capacity to adapt regular operational plans to the unexpected character of hilly locations, ensuring that troops are not only prepared to fight but also capable of navigating the physical hurdles they will face.

One of the most difficult features of mountain combat is the quick and often severe weather fluctuations. These climatic factors can have an impact on troop visibility, movement, and health. To reduce these dangers, effective mountain warfare tactics must include contingencies for rapid weather changes, like as weather forecasts and historical climatic data, in the planning phase.

Given the complexities of mountainous terrain, deploying soldiers and fighting the adversary necessitates specialized techniques that take verticality and isolation into account. Units must be prepared for confrontations at many levels, such as air assaults and cliff-side operations. Tactics must be versatile, allowing units to quickly switch from travel to combat mode. Preparations for enemy contact should include the construction of high-ground vantage sites and the use of topography for cover and concealment.

Mobility in Mountainous Terrain

Vertical impediments are widespread in mountain warfare and pose serious threats to movement and safety. Units must be taught in strategies for analyzing and safely overcoming these features, whether through climbing, technical equipment, or alternative routes. The ability to quickly and successfully navigate these hurdles can mean the difference between a successful operation and a tactical failure.

Understanding and selecting the optimal routes is critical for keeping an operation running well and avoiding enemy detection. Routes are classed according to their difficulty and tactical value, which guides decision-making in route design. This classification aids in resource allocation, movement phase planning, and developing realistic deadlines for achieving goals.

Physical fitness and adaptation to high altitudes are essential components in mountain warfare. Soldiers must go through intense physical training designed to meet the difficulties of operating in high-altitude conditions. This comprises both general fitness and specific training to improve climbing stamina and resistance to altitude sickness. Effective acclimatization techniques guarantee that soldiers are physically capable of carrying out operations without experiencing weariness or health problems, ensuring operational success throughout the war.

By focusing on these important areas, military planners can improve the performance of their troops in mountainous terrains, ensuring that they are not only equipped to meet physical challenges but also to capitalize on the tactical advantages provided by the mountains. This comprehensive approach to planning and mobility lays the groundwork for successful operations in one of the world's most difficult battle zones.

Equipment for Mountain Operations

In mountain operations, the correct gear is more than just convenient; it is essential for survival and success. Choosing, using, and maintaining primary climbing equipment is critical. This includes specialist footwear, clothing designed for changing weather conditions, sturdy backpacks, cold-weather sleeping systems, and navigation instruments such as compasses and GPS devices. Each piece of gear must be strong enough to resist the severe mountain environment while remaining lightweight and efficient so as not to hamper mobility.

The emphasis here is on non-technical equipment that facilitates general mountaineering activity. This includes hydration devices, energy-efficient cooking systems, and first-aid kits specifically built for high-altitude illnesses and injuries.

Planning and Execution of Movements

Effective movement in high terrain begins with a thorough terrain examination. This analysis guides the selection of movement tactics appropriate for various types of terrain, ranging from gentle slopes to rugged cliffs. Units must be able to evaluate topographical maps and aerial images in order to plan their paths, avoiding natural impediments and maximizing cover.

Different types of terrain create unique problems that necessitate careful consideration for mobility and planning. For example, modest slopes (Class 1) may allow for quick mobility while requiring limited technical abilities, whereas steeper inclines (Class 2 and 3) may involve the use of hands for balance and minor climbing. Higher grades of terrain, which include steep and exposed approaches, necessitate careful planning to guarantee that troops can move safely and effectively without jeopardizing their operational capabilities. Commanders must understand these characteristics in order to efficiently allocate resources, organize moves, and anticipate the obstacles that their forces will experience in the field.

Units' operational preparedness and tactical effectiveness in hilly situations can be improved by combining extensive equipment knowledge with strategic movement planning. This method assures that Rangers are not only skilled, but also have the requisite equipment and strategies to dominate in high-altitude and hard terrain missions.

TECHNIQUES FOR EFFECTIVE CLIMBING AND RESCUE

In the complicated tapestry of modern military operations, climbing skills have evolved as not only helpful but also necessary, particularly when operating in difficult, mountainous terrains. The geographic distribution of potential conflict zones in today's geopolitical landscape frequently includes locations where classic movement techniques are ineffective. Vertical mobility mastery can provide strategic dominance by allowing forces to navigate and secure previously inaccessible terrain, resulting in important tactical advantages such as surprise and an elevated observation stance.

Climbing operations can be essential in obtaining an advantage during conflicts, allowing units to move quickly and safely up steep inclines and outmanoeuvre opponents. This capacity is especially important in mountain warfare, where height and the ability to maneuver vertically frequently determine the result of battle. As a result, mastering climbing skills is more than simply an asset; it is essential for sustaining the efficacy and diversity of a modern fighting force.

Rescue Operations

The field of rescue operations inside military maneuvers is equally important and difficult. The unpredictable nature of military operations, along with hard terrain and the high risk of fighting, needs a strong capability for swift and effective rescue. These missions are critical not only for the recovery and medical care of injured people, but also for the unit's morale and combat readiness.

Training for rescue operations entails a thorough understanding of technical skills and equipment. Soldiers must be able to use a variety of rescue equipment, which may include complex rigging systems, stretchers, and emergency medical supplies. They must also be trained to make quick choices under pressure, as rescue missions frequently occur under enemy fire or in hazardous environmental conditions.

Specialized training modules are created to provide Rangers with the abilities needed to undertake high-risk rescues in a range of combat scenarios. These training programs emphasize speedy casualty extraction, safe and efficient patient transport, and injury stabilization until further medical attention can be provided. The goal is to ensure that each member of a unit is not just a capable warrior but also a competent rescuer, ready to provide essential support and potentially save lives in the midst of combat.

This dual emphasis on climbing and rescue operations highlights their interconnected nature in modern military strategy, where the capacity to reach and retrieve, ascend and aid, is as important as any fighting skill. In this light, climbing and rescue operations training, equipment, and execution are more than merely operational components; they are vital cornerstones of modern military readiness.

Task Organization and Team Roles

Military mountaineering and rescue missions require rigorous team organization to optimize operational efficiency and effectiveness. Each unit within a Ranger platoon is organized to complete certain activities that are critical to the success of mountain operations. Casualty evacuation teams, reconnaissance teams, and dedicated security teams are all made up of personnel who have received specialized training for their specific roles.

1. **Casualty Evacuation Teams**: These teams play an important role in situations where soldiers are injured and must be taken to a medical facility swiftly and safely. The crews are outfitted with medical supplies and evacuation equipment such as litters and ropes that are specifically built for speedy descent and extraction in difficult terrain.
2. **Reconnaissance Teams**: These teams are frequently the first to interact with the landscape, assessing the safety and passability of routes. They are outfitted with advanced navigation tools and taught to identify potential risks, enemy positions, and the best paths for the main unit to take.
3. **Security Teams**: Tasked with the protection of the climbing and rescue teams, these units are

responsible for maintaining a defensive perimeter, ensuring that the operation can proceed without interference from enemy forces or environmental hazards.

Roles and Responsibilities

Within these teams, each member has a clearly defined role that is vital to the unit's overall success. These positions are intended to use individual talents and specialties to improve team performance.

1. **Lead Climbers**: Typically the most experienced climbers, lead climbers navigate the initial and most challenging portions of the ascent. Their role is to establish the route, place protection gear, and make critical decisions regarding the path and pace of the climb.
2. **Belayers**: Belayers are strategically positioned to control the safety ropes that are attached to climbers. Their major task is to keep the rope tensioned and adjusted as needed to avoid falls. They must be extremely vigilant and prepared to react quickly to changes in the climber's condition.
3. **Rescue Personnel**: These individuals are casualty evacuation team specialists who have received training in advanced first aid, trauma treatment, and the use of complex evacuation equipment. They are equipped to provide urgent care in the field and oversee the safe extraction of wounded in often hazardous settings.

Each team member is also cross-trained to fulfill several duties as needed, which improves the unit's adaptability and resilience. The flexibility in responsibilities ensures that the team can continue to function even if some members are incapacitated or otherwise engaged.

The performance of these teams is dependent not just on the individual abilities of their members, but also on their ability to work as a cohesive one. Regular exercises, simulations, and after-action evaluations are crucial for improving team strategy and ensuring that each member understands their own and their colleagues' duties. This high level of readiness distinguishes Rangers in alpine operations and allows them to carry out complex tasks under difficult conditions.

Rescue Equipment and Techniques

The efficiency of military rescues, particularly in challenging terrains such as mountainous environments, heavily relies on the quality and adaptability of the equipment used. The standard litter system employed by Rangers is engineered for versatility and effectiveness under the extreme conditions often encountered during missions. Components of the Standard Litter System includes:

- **Stretchers**: Made of lightweight, robust materials such as low-density polyethylene, it can tolerate severe temperatures and hard handling. The stretchers have solid brass grommets and strong nylon webbing for secure attachment points.
- **Slings and Carabiners**: These vital components are built of materials with great tensile strength that can withstand heavy loads. Slings often have a tensile strength of up to 10,000 pounds, whereas carabiners are made of locking steel with a tensile strength of roughly 9,000 pounds.
- **Tow Straps**: Included to facilitate the transport and maneuvering of the stretcher, these straps have a lower tensile strength but are crucial for quick adjustments and movements during rescue operations.

Deployment and Usage of Rescue Equipment

Deploying rescue equipment efficiently necessitates not just a comprehension of its functionality, but also the capacity to tailor its application to the scenario at hand. The standard litter system's adaptability allows it to be used in a number of scenarios, including high-angle rescues and quick evacuations.

1. **Setting up the Litter**: The setup process begins with unfolding the stretcher and attaching horizontal and vertical lift slings. Depending on the nature of the rescue, the stretcher can be prepared for horizontal or vertical extraction using the appropriate sling configurations.
2. **Adapting to Terrain**: In hilly areas, where vertical extractions are more common, the vertical lift

configuration is preferable. This entails attaching the stretcher with a vertical lift sling threaded through grommets located along its length, ensuring that the casualty's weight is uniformly distributed.

Loading Procedures for Casualties

Handling casualties with utmost care is paramount, and the method of loading them onto the stretcher must minimize movement to avoid exacerbating injuries. The standard rescue kit includes tools and instructions for two primary loading methods:

1. Logroll Method:
- Position the stretcher adjacent to the casualty, ensuring it is aligned with their body.
- Carefully roll the casualty onto their side, then slide the stretcher underneath them.
- Gently roll the casualty onto the stretcher, securing them with straps and ensuring they are centered for balance and comfort.

2. Slide Method:
- Ideal for confined spaces or when injuries prevent rolling, this method requires positioning the stretcher at the head or foot of the casualty.
- One rescuer supports the casualty's head and shoulders while two others use the straps to slide the stretcher beneath the casualty.

Each procedure is intended to guarantee that the casualty is loaded securely and safely, with a low chance of further injury. The approach used is determined on the casualty's state, the surrounding surroundings, and the urgency of the situation.

Rangers are equipped to carry out high-stakes rescue missions effectively after receiving rigorous, systematic training and a complete understanding of both the equipment and procedures. This preparedness means that even in the most difficult conditions, the chances of successful recovery are maximized, demonstrating the Rangers' dedication to leaving no one behind.

Essential Gear for Advanced Operations

Advanced climbing activities necessitate specific equipment that allows Rangers to perform in harsh situations and diverse terrains. This section discusses the important equipment required for such missions, with a focus on technical climbing and high-angle rescue efforts.

1. **Technical Climbing Kits**: These kits are designed to help climbers in vertical or near-vertical areas when typical hiking and climbing methods are insufficient. They usually feature dynamic ropes, customized harnesses, sophisticated carabiners, and climbing helmets. The gear in these kits is intended to support not just physical climbing, but also safety measures that safeguard climbers from falls and other hazards. Dynamic ropes, for example, are designed to absorb the energy of a fall, lowering the risk to the climber.

2. **High-Angle Equipment**: High-angle operations entail rescues and movements on steep inclines when normal approaches are impractical. These surgeries require pulleys, vertical lift tripods, and specialized stretchers. This equipment is essential for securely traveling and rescuing in high-angle settings, as it provides secure and robust solutions that can be used in restricted or hazardous environments.

Utilization of Specialized Kits

Different kits are designed for specific scenarios, each enabling Rangers to maximize their effectiveness in various operational contexts. Understanding the application of these kits helps in planning and executing missions with precision and safety.

1. High-Angle Mountaineering Kit (HAMK):

- *Usage*: Designed for operations on steep, non-icy terrains where ropes and anchors are used extensively. The kit includes tools for securing routes, aiding in vertical climbs, and ensuring the safety of personnel during such climbs.
- *Components*: Includes harnesses, a range of carabiners (locking and non-locking), and ropes specifically suited for rugged terrain climbing, where flexibility and durability are paramount.

2. Assault Climber Team Kit (ACTK):

- *Application*: Used by trained assault climber teams to establish routes that other personnel can navigate safely. This kit allows for the rapid deployment of rope installations in hostile environments.
- *Details*: Features high-strength, lightweight equipment such as mechanical ascenders and rock protection gear, which are essential for establishing secure climbing paths under combat conditions.

3. Snow and Ice Mobility Kit (SIMK):

- *Context*: Essential for operations in environments dominated by snow and ice, where movement is hindered by slippery surfaces and avalanche risk.
- *Kit Contents*: Includes crampons, ice axes, and snowshoes, which enhance mobility and safety. Additional tools like avalanche transceivers and probes are vital for quick location and recovery in the event of an avalanche.

Each piece of equipment in these kits has been carefully selected to provide maximum functionality and compatibility with other gear, ensuring Rangers are prepared to face the demands of mountain combat. Rangers' capacity to operate efficiently in diverse and hard conditions is enhanced by incorporating these specific tools into their normal operating procedures, allowing them to maintain preparedness and operational supremacy in hilly terrain.

CHAPTER 11: URBAN COMBAT STRATEGIES

STRATEGIES FOR URBAN WARFARE PREPARATION

In the area of modern military strategy, urban warfare is a complicated and more prevalent arena that calls into question traditional fighting techniques. Urban areas, with their dense population centers and sophisticated infrastructures, require a paradigm shift from traditional warfare encounters. Urban settings are more than just backdrops for military operations; they are dynamic battlefields requiring acute strategic planning and adaptation.

Military operations in these locations are complicated because to the multidimensional landscape, which encompasses not only the horizontal spread of a metropolis but also its vertical stratification. High-rise structures, subterranean corridors, and densely packed residential areas form a multidimensional battlefield that impacts visibility, mobility, and the effectiveness of various weapon systems.

The volatility and complexity of urban environments necessitate rigorous planning to improve operational performance and reduce risks. Preparing for urban battle entails more than just accumulating superior weapons or troops; it also requires a thorough grasp of the urban geography, effective communication methods, and the integration of multiple military forces.

Training exercises designed to mimic urban environments can be useful. These drills should include scenarios that simulate the possible chaos and civilian presence in urban battles, ensuring that soldiers understand urban navigation, building clearance, and engagement regulations that minimize collateral damage while maximizing tactical gain.

Strategic Importance of Urban Areas

Urban centers are frequently the epicenters of political, economic, and cultural activity. This makes them important places of interest in both conventional and asymmetric combat. Control over small localities can have a considerable impact on the larger battle, influencing national morale and economic stability in the region. The symbolic significance of metropolitan centers can also increase the psychological impact of military dominance or triumph, both locally and internationally.

Furthermore, metropolitan locations frequently serve as hubs for infrastructure such as transportation networks, communication nodes, and utilities, all of which are critical assets in modern warfare. Controlling these can provide major operational advantages while disrupting the enemy's capabilities.

Characteristics of Urban Terrain

The geography of metropolitan regions poses distinct obstacles and opportunities for military operations. The great density of buildings and tight alleys limit visibility and movement, making street-to-street and house-to-house warfare difficult undertakings. Verticality is critical; rooftops, windows, and underground networks provide both observation points and possible dangers.

Furthermore, the presence of civilian infrastructure in battle zones complicates the use of weapons due to the significant potential of collateral damage. Precision in combat operations and increased situational awareness are required to avoid non-combatant casualties and structural devastation, which could spark public outrage or international condemnation.

To summarize, urban warfare entails more than just tactical engagement; it necessitates a comprehensive approach that incorporates environmental awareness, skilled use of technology, and the ability to adapt to fast changing conditions. Effective planning, a thorough understanding of urban characteristics, and smart use of urban centers are critical for operational success and mission fulfillment in these complex contexts.

Planning for Urban Warfare

Urban operations require a comprehensive strategy that smoothly incorporates offensive, defensive, and stability operations. This integration is critical in a setting where the distinction between fighting and non-combat zones is blurred, and the civilian population is inextricably linked to the combatants.

1. **Offensive Operations**: In an urban setting, they are frequently defined by the requirement to capture or secure critical places within the city, such as government buildings, communication centers, and transportation nodes. The tight quarters and diverse topography of urban situations necessitate precise, regulated tactics that reduce collateral damage while increasing impact on enemy forces.

2. **Defensive Operations**: Urban settings offer various defensive benefits, including the ability to fortify positions within buildings and use the city's natural density to impede enemy mobility. Defensive operations in urban warfare also include managing access points, erecting checkpoints, and employing surveillance to preserve territorial control.

3. **Stability Operations**: These efforts are crucial for preserving order and assisting civilian populations during and after hostilities. In urban warfare, stability operations may include providing humanitarian relief, restoring key services, and maintaining civil order by police activities or military presence.

Several factors uniquely influence the conduct of military operations in urban environments:

- **Terrain Dominance**: Controlling high-rise buildings or other elevated positions can result in major tactical advantages, such as improved visibility and fire positions. The capacity to dominate the urban terrain can control the flow of the operation and have a substantial impact on its success.

- **Logistical Support**: Because of the environmental constraints that urban enterprises face, considerable logistical preparation is required. The density of buildings, combined with the risk for infrastructure damage, can interrupt supply lines. It is essential to hold a sufficient amount of ammunition, food, medical supplies, and reinforcements.

- **Importance of Civilian Support**: Gaining the support of the local populace can be critical in urban warfare. Civilians can contribute critical intelligence, help operations run more smoothly, and ultimately impact the outcome of the fight. Winning hearts and minds can be as vital as winning tactical battles.

Environmental Considerations

The distinctive features of the urban environment play a crucial part in operational planning:

1. **Weather and Climate**: Urban locations can generate microclimates with different weather patterns. For example, the heat island effect can change the local climate in a metropolis. Adverse weather conditions, such as heavy rain or snow, can compound these impacts, reducing vision, movement, and the efficacy of some technology.

2. **Terrain Variability**: The urban landscape is characterized by its diversity. A single city block may contain a combination of open spaces, densely packed residential units, industrial regions, and subsurface networks. This degree of diversity necessitates adaptable tactics and equipment designed for a variety of conditions.

3. **Urban Density**: High population density and physical density of structures present considerable issues, ranging from logistical complications to greater collateral damage risk. To preserve operational legitimacy and support in dense urban situations, force must be applied with precision and damage control measures increased.

In conclusion, preparing for urban warfare necessitates an awareness of the complexities and dynamics of urban surroundings. Commanders must be flexible yet decisive, incorporating a diverse set of military weapons and tactics tailored to the specific problems of urban conflict.

Unit Composition and Roles

Organizing units for urban operations necessitates a thorough awareness of the numerous and intricate functions that various military elements play in such locations. The appropriate organization of these units is critical for operational success and the safety of both fighters and noncombatants.

1. **Infantry Units**: These provide the foundation of urban activities. Infantry units are largely tasked for navigating across urban terrain, securing buildings, and engaging enemy forces at close range. Their training is largely focused on room clearance procedures, urban patrolling, and ensuring security in a densely populated area.

2. **Special Operations Forces (SOF)**: SOF units bring a level of precision, agility, and specialized skills that are crucial for targeted operations such as hostage rescue, high-value target extraction, and gathering intelligence in hostile urban settings. Their ability to operate discreetly in civilian-populated areas is invaluable.

3. **Civil Affairs Units**: These units are crucial in coordinating with civilian populations and local governments. They aim to reduce civilian involvement with military activities, manage civilian expectations, and promote humanitarian assistance and civil-military operations, all of which are critical to sustaining local support.

4. **Engineers and Military Police**: Engineers are critical to mobility and countermobility operations. They help with breaching operations, fortification construction, and the removal of common impediments in urban situations. Military police aid to maintain order, direct displaced populations, and control traffic, thereby preventing logistical bottlenecks during operations.

Integration of Specialized Units

The integration of specialized units such as armor, artillery, and chemical units requires careful consideration due to the complexities of urban combat.

1. **Armor Units**: While armor units have typically been regarded as less effective in near urban terrain due to navigational difficulties and susceptibility to ambushes, they can provide invaluable direct fire support and better protection for ground troops. Their deployment must be carefully planned to maximize their capabilities while limiting their drawbacks in constrained urban environments.

2. **Artillery Units**: Given the possibility of collateral damage, using artillery in urban warfare requires careful planning. Precision-guided munitions and modified fire regulations are required to reduce accidental fatalities. Artillery can be useful in dislodging entrenched enemies and providing fire support in sparsely populated areas or in preparation for an assault.

The task organization for urban operations must be versatile and fluid, with a command structure capable of bringing together these disparate units into a cohesive operational force. This integration enables a multidimensional approach to urban fighting, which is required given the complexity of the terrain and the numerous obstacles it poses. Each unit's distinct capabilities must be properly used to dominate the urban battlefield, achieve strategic goals, and reduce overall danger to both military troops and civilians.

Interaction with Non-Combatants

In the area of urban warfare, the interaction between armed personnel and civilian populations is unavoidable. Effective civil-military operations (CMO) are critical for not only earning the support of local residents but also lowering the likelihood of civilian losses, which can have a significant impact on overall mission success and long-term stability in the region. Engagement Strategies includes:

- **Communication and Collaboration**: Open lines of communication with local politicians and community leaders will help to build confidence and collaboration. This collaboration helps to better understand the demands of the civilian population and incorporate those into operational planning.

- **Humanitarian Assistance**: Provide emergency relief services such as medical care, food, drink, and shelter. These activities not only alleviate human suffering, but also reflect the military forces' good intentions, combating any negative propaganda from opposing troops.

Rules of Engagement (ROE)

Because urban situations are complex, ROEs must be explicit enough to offer soldiers with clear instructions while also being adaptive enough to respond to fast changing scenarios. ROEs must strike a balance between effective military operations and minimizing civilian harm.

1. Development and Implementation:
- *Clarity and Specificity*: ROEs should clearly define what is considered a legitimate target and under what circumstances soldiers can engage. This clarity helps prevent incidents that could escalate into larger conflicts or lead to civilian casualties.
- *Adaptability*: As the urban environment changes or new intelligence emerges, ROEs must be promptly revised and presented to all workers. Commanders can make real-time judgments based on the present operational realities because to the flexibility of ROEs.

2. Training and Dissemination:
- *Scenario-Based Training*: Soldiers should get rigorous training that simulates a wide range of urban combat scenarios, including those involving civilians. This training should also focus on the legal and ethical ramifications of their acts under the ROEs.
- *Continuous Education*: Updates to ROEs and any lessons learned from the field should be systematically integrated into regular training cycles to ensure all personnel are informed and prepared.

3. Accountability Mechanisms:
- *Monitoring and Reporting*: Implement systems for monitoring adherence to ROEs and for reporting and investigating any breaches. Such mechanisms ensure accountability and help maintain the ethical standards expected of military personnel.

The integration of robust civil-military operations with well-defined, adaptive ROEs is important to urban combat strategy. They not only aid operational success, but also uphold the moral and ethical standards demanded of military members, fostering long-term peace and stability in urban areas.

TECHNIQUES FOR SECURING ROOMS AND REACTING TO INDIRECT THREATS

Room clearance is an essential ability in modern military operations, particularly for troops like the Rangers, who frequently face close-quarter combat scenarios. The capacity to clear rooms quickly and safely is critical to the success of any mission in urban or enclosed areas. This task is vital not only for neutralizing threats, but also for protecting noncombatants who may be ensnared in such high-risk zones.

During operations, units may face the problem of clearing rooms suspected of containing enemy combatants. The presence of hostile forces as well as noncombatants complicates these scenarios. The actions must be carried out with precision and care to minimize civilian losses while effectively neutralizing threats. This dynamic necessitates well-coordinated tactics and strict adherence to the rules of engagement, highlighting the importance of rigorous training and discipline among the Rangers.

Before a room clearing operation begins, it is critical to properly arrange support and security personnel. These units offer critical cover and establish a secure environment in which the assault force can function efficiently. Proper location isolates the target room from exterior reinforcements and restricts the movement of enemy troops attempting to flee or counterattack.

The success of a room clearing operation is heavily dependent on the leadership at the helm. The unit leader must maintain a command post that provides a strategic overview of the action while ensuring safety. From this vantage position, the leader may make crucial decisions, guide the flow of operations, and make real-time adjustments depending on team feedback and changing conditions in the room. The leader's ability to command and control the situation is critical to ensuring that the clearing team can carry out its duties quickly while adjusting to any unexpected changes in the danger environment.

This preparatory phase lays the groundwork for a successful room clearing operation, since knowing roles, command directives, and the tactical relevance of each step impacts the engagement's outcome.

Entry Techniques

Effective room clearing begins with controlled and quick entry procedures that reduce exposure to potential dangers while increasing the element of surprise. The entry operation is frequently preceded by the use of grenades, with strict adherence to the rules of engagement to assure both the effectiveness and legality of the action. A fragmentation, concussion, or stun grenade can be employed in high-intensity fighting. The grenade is quickly "cooked off" (detonated in a controlled manner) before being thrown into the room, followed by an immediate "FRAG OUT" announcement to notify team members. This technique is crucial for confusing enemy inhabitants and restricting their ability to reply effectively.

Clearing Methodology

Once the grenade has been launched and detonated, the clearing crew enters. The first two team members arrive nearly simultaneously, dividing up to cover additional area. The first soldier moves to the left or right, taking the path of least resistance, swiftly claiming a corner of the room to control the space. This soldier checks for and neutralizes imminent threats as he moves forward.

The second soldier enters quickly after the first, heading in the other direction to ensure complete sector control. This systematic strategy enables the squad to effectively destroy threats while avoiding overlapping fields of fire, which could lead to fratricide.

Sequential entrance guarantees that each team member is assigned a specific sector to control, with their movements and actions guided by pre-established strategies. This methodical approach to the room allows the team to immediately create a strong foothold, from which they may further command the situation.

Each member of the clearing team is trained to attack and neutralize obvious threats with precision-aimed fire while minimizing damage to noncombatants and property. Clear communication among team members is critical during the admission and clearance process. It guarantees that every area of the room is properly covered and that any possible dangers are addressed before moving on to the next phase of the process.

The clearing team leader coordinates the crew's movements and actions, ensuring that all areas of the room are investigated and secured. Once the room is pronounced clear, the team commander signals the operation's success to the unit leader, who then decides whether to clear more rooms or consolidate and reorganize.

This organized method to room clearing allows Rangers to efficiently control any environment, assuring mission success while upholding the greatest levels of safety and efficiency.

Post-Clearing Procedures

- **Room Security**: Once a room has been effectively cleared, the immediate next step is to secure the space to prevent enemy troops from re-entering and to ensure a safe environment for future operations. This includes clearly identifying the entry point in accordance with the unit's standard operating procedures (SOP). This marking could include actual tags, particular signs, or other markers as specified by the unit's protocol to ensure that any member of the unit can see the status of the area at a glance.

- **Assessment and Reporting**: After securing the space, the clearance team undertakes a rapid but thorough assessment of any materials, weapons, or intelligence that may be tactically useful. This assessment also includes looking for potential hazards or booby traps left behind that could threaten the unit or impede future operations. Once the room has been certified secure and all valuable information has been acquired, the team leader will report up the chain of command. This report provides the room's status, any battles that took place, the presence of enemy or noncombatant casualties, and any intelligence collected.

- **Reorganization**: Following the secure and report phase, the unit reorganizes. This phase is critical to ensuring operational continuity and readiness. Ammunition inspections, minor equipment repairs, medical exams, and redistribution of necessary supplies among team members are all part of the reorganization process. It also entails establishing a defensive perimeter, if the operational tempo allows, to prepare for any enemy counterattacks or to continue clearing operations in the region.

During this phase, each team member is assigned clear duties and responsibilities, ensuring that the unit can swiftly restore full operational capability. The platoon leader or unit commander evaluates overall readiness and determines the next moves, such as further advancing, holding positions, or withdrawing from the place. This structured method guarantees that the unit retains its tactical edge and readiness post-clearance, ready for any further operations or unanticipated developments.

Reacting to Indirect Fire

When a unit comes under indirect fire, such as artillery or mortar rounds, fast action is critical to reducing losses and disorientation. When incoming bullets are detected—as indicated by the call "INCOMING" or the distinct sound of impacts—the reaction process is activated immediately.

- **Dismounted Response**: If cover is not immediately accessible, soldiers must drop to the prone position or run to the nearest cover that protects against shrapnel and blasts. This quick response is vital to survival and must be carried out with meticulous accuracy.

- **Mounted Response**: For troops in vehicles, the first response is for all vehicle commanders to echo the incoming alarm via communication equipment. Drivers must respond by relocating their vehicles out of the identified impact area, following pre-determined routes that consider the fastest exit from the threat zone. Vehicle commanders ensure that all hatches are closed and people are buttoned up for maximum protection.

Movement to Safety

Post-initial evasion, the unit must regroup at a pre-determined rally point that is outside the effective range of the indirect fire.

- **Dismounted Movement**: Soldiers move swiftly, maintaining unit cohesion and utilizing covered and concealed routes to the rally point. The speed and stealth of this movement are paramount to prevent further casualties.
- **Mounted Movement**: Vehicles travel to the rally point under the guidance of the unit leader, who gives specific directions via radio. The choice of path and speed is determined by topography, adversary capabilities, and the level of vehicle protection against indirect fire.

Post-Indirect Fire Action

Once safely at the rally point, the unit undertakes several critical actions to regain operational capability and prepare for potential follow-on missions or further enemy action.

- **Accounting and Reorganization**: The unit leader conducts a roll call to check that all troops are present and evaluates the unit's combat efficiency following the battle. This includes assessing casualties, equipment status, and ammo levels. Quick reorganization efforts include delegating jobs to handle any security concerns and planning for prospective counter-moves or sustained mission objectives.
- **Communication**: The unit leader interacts with higher headquarters to report the indirect fire incident, including unit status, losses (if any), and preliminary estimates of enemy intent based on the pattern and efficacy of the fire. This report is critical for coordinating larger unit reactions, revising tactical plans, and notifying higher command about the situation on the ground.

In all actions, the unit's ability to remain calm, react promptly, and follow trained procedures determines the effectiveness of the response to indirect fire, underpinning the resilience and preparedness essential for operating in hostile environments.

CHAPTER 12: AQUATIC OPERATIONAL TACTICS

CONSTRUCTION OF MAKESHIFT AQUATIC VEHICLES

In the complicated theater of modern military operations, strategic deployment of improvised aquatic vehicles is critical. These impromptu solutions increase ground forces' reach beyond water barriers, giving both strategic surprise and operational flexibility. They are critical in situations where traditional tactics are either unfeasible or unavailable, helping units to sustain momentum in dynamic battle settings.

This section looks at the many homemade aquatic vehicles used by armed troops, with a focus on two main types: rope bridges and poncho rafts. Each has a specific purpose, ranging from stealthy infiltrations to critical gap crossings during combat. Their design and deployment demonstrate a thorough understanding of resourcefulness and adaptability, both of which are essential characteristics in unconventional and guerilla warfare.

Preparing for Waterborne Operations
Proper preparation is foundational to the effective use of improvised aquatic vehicles. Personnel must be equipped to handle the physical demands and hazards of waterborne operations. The following points explain the most important aspects of gear and uniform configuration:

1. Uniform Configuration: Ensure that pant legs are unbloused to prevent water from being trapped inside, which can weigh down a soldier. Tops should be fully zipped and collars fastened to minimize water entry and reduce drag.

2. Securing Equipment:
- *Swimmer Safety Line*: A vital component, the swimmer safety line should be tied using an around-the-waist bowline knot, extending with an end-of-line bowline at arm's length. Carabiners are attached at strategic points to facilitate quick rescue operations if necessary.
- *Field Load Carrier (FLC)*: The FLC should be unzipped to prevent it from snagging and to allow for quick access to essential gear.

Safety lines are more than just a precaution; they are necessary for sustaining unit cohesion and ensuring that all members are accounted for during crossings. The proper arrangement of equipment improves mobility and safety, lowering the chance of entanglement or loss of important supplies. This configuration is critical for sustaining operational preparedness and effectiveness, even in the demanding conditions of maritime operations.

Rangers ensure they are ready to carry out any mission across water obstacles effectively and securely by meticulously preparing and adhering to these rules. This amount of preparation demonstrates the professionalism and capability demanded of elite groups like the Rangers, allowing them to function effectively in a variety of demanding environments.

Construction of Rope Bridges
Rope bridges, an essential component of modern tactical operations, are critical assets in clandestine operations across difficult terrain, particularly water impediments. These temporary constructions are used to enable the silent movement of forces, improving operational stealth and strategic surprise. They are frequently employed in situations where standard crossing methods could jeopardize the mission's secrecy or where structural bridges are unavailable.

Covert gap crossings are precisely prepared operations that allow for the undetected passage of physical barriers. These activities are critical in retaining the element of surprise, which is required for the success of many military confrontations. The ability to maneuver silently across gaps not only shields the unit from adversary discovery, but also places it well for future activities.

Constructing a rope bridge requires coordination among various team members, each with specific roles and responsibilities:

1. **Lead Safety Swimmer and Farside Lifeguard (Ranger #1)**: Ensures the safety of the team members crossing and secures the far side of the crossing point.
2. **Rope Swimmer (Ranger #2)**: Swims across the obstacle with the rope, establishing the initial link between the two sides.
3. **Nearside Lifeguard (Ranger #3)**: Secures the starting point and assists the last members across the bridge.

Each team member has distinct duties that must be performed with precision to ensure the bridge's successful and covert construction:

- **BTC (Bridge Team Commander, Ranger #4)**: Oversees the entire operation, from the initial setup to the final member crossing. The BTC is also responsible for the strategic placement of the rope and ensuring all safety measures are adhered to.
- **Rope Pullers (Rangers #5 and #6)**: Responsible for pulling the rope tight and securing it, ensuring the bridge's stability and readiness for crossing.

The construction of a rope bridge requires specialized equipment to ensure both the efficiency of the build and the safety of the personnel involved:

- **Ropes and Carabiners**: Essential for creating the actual bridge. Carabiners are used to secure the rope at anchor points and to attach personal equipment.
- **Safety Lines and Life Preservers**: Crucial for the safety of the swimmers and other team members working near or in the water.
- **Utility Ropes**: Used for additional securing and tightening of the rope bridge.

Each piece of equipment must be thoroughly tested and prepped prior to deployment, since the reliability of the tools employed might determine the success of the operation. The deliberate deployment and efficient use of these resources demonstrate the high level of preparedness and competence required of Rangers involved in such high-stakes missions.

Execution Phases of Rope Bridge Construction

The first phase of building a rope bridge entails extensive preparations and rigorous planning. This stage is critical for ensuring that the operational objectives are in line with the unit's tactical capabilities. It entails careful topographical mapping, understanding water currents and environmental variables, and strategically selecting the bridge location to optimize concealment while minimizing exposure to enemy observation.

Maintaining security during the construction phase is critical. The team must be alert to react to enemy contact at any time. Procedures for immediately safeguarding the facility and responding to threats should be thoroughly practiced. This includes the deployment of security teams upstream and downstream to monitor for enemy activities and secure the safety of the construction workers.

The construction of the rope bridge follows a sequence of well-defined steps:

- **Setting Up Anchor Points**: Identifying and securing strong anchor points on both sides of the crossing. This is often the duty of the team's most technically capable members, who must guarantee that the anchor points can withstand the weight and stress of the bridge when fully loaded.
- **Securing Ropes**: Ropes are then extended across the gap, secured at the anchor points using appropriate knots that allow for quick release but also provide stability during crossing.
- **Adjusting Tension and Alignment**: The ropes must be pulled tight and aligned correctly to ensure the

bridge is stable and can support the crossing without excessive swaying or sagging.

Maintaining noise control is critical for avoiding discovery. All team members must be trained to operate as silently as possible, using hand signals and minimizing any movement that could cause noise. The crossing location must be secured with disguised stations to monitor and offer cover as needed. This includes establishing temporary observation posts that may detect prospective threats while concealing the team's presence.

Utilization of Poncho Rafts in Tactical Operations

Poncho rafts, which are frequently used in military operations to traverse water obstacles, provide a makeshift but effective mode of conveyance across water bodies. This section investigates the strategic use of poncho rafts, focusing on their role in maintaining operational secrecy and reducing logistical costs in locations where conventional boats may not be practicable or available.

The decision to use poncho rafts is contingent upon several environmental conditions that influence their practicality and effectiveness:

- **Water Current and Depth**: Poncho rafts are most suitable for calm and shallow waters where the risk of capsizing is minimal.
- **Availability of Materials**: The feasibility of constructing poncho rafts depends on the availability of essential materials like ponchos, ropes, and rucksacks.

Constructing a poncho raft involves a series of steps that transform standard military equipment into a functional raft. Here's how Rangers typically assemble a poncho raft:

1. Preparation of Materials:
- Lay two military ponchos flat on the ground, ensuring that the hoods are tightly sealed to prevent water ingress.
- Arrange equipment such as rucksacks and weapons centrally between the ponchos, using them to provide structural integrity and flotation.

2. Assembling the Raft:
- Place poles or rifles parallel within the poncho, creating a frame that helps maintain the raft's shape.
- Fold the sides of the poncho over the equipment and poles, starting from the edges and rolling towards the center to encapsulate the gear securely.

3. Securing the Structure:
- Use utility cords or boot laces to tie off the ends of the ponchos, ensuring the contents are tightly wrapped and the poncho material is secured against water entry.
- Employ additional ropes to bind the raft longitudinally, enhancing its stability and load-bearing capacity.

4. Final Adjustments and Waterproofing:
- Test the raft's buoyancy in shallow water, adjusting the tightness of the ropes and the distribution of weight as necessary.
- Double-check all knots and seals for waterproof integrity to ensure that no equipment is compromised during the crossing.

Once constructed, the deployment of poncho rafts involves strategic considerations:
- **Launching**: Identify a discreet launch point that offers both cover and ease of access to the water.
- **Crossing**: Navigate the raft with paddles or your hands, adopting a low profile to avoid discovery.
- **Landing and Extraction**: Upon reaching the opposite bank, quickly disassemble the raft and secure all equipment, leaving no trace of the crossing to maintain operational secrecy.

The building and use of poncho rafts demonstrates Rangers' versatility and inventiveness under field settings.

Rangers can easily cross water obstacles without the need for specialist equipment, keeping the element of surprise in tactical operations. This section offers a complete instruction to creating and using poncho rafts, specifically designed for the competent and imaginative character of elite military troops operating in challenging environments.

NAVIGATION AND TACTICAL WATER MOVEMENTS

Navigation and tactical movement expertise during maritime operations are vital skill sets for today's military forces, especially for units like the Rangers, which must operate effectively in a variety of situations. This chapter goes into critical waterborne methods such as capsize procedures, advanced navigation techniques, efficient river movements, and secure landing tactics, providing Rangers with the knowledge they need to improve operational performance and reduce hazards in aquatic circumstances.

Capsize Recovery Techniques

Understanding and carrying out capsize drills are critical in protecting both personnel and equipment. These drills train Rangers for unexpected scenarios in which quick and coordinated actions might make the difference between life and death, as well as the preservation or loss of important equipment.

Capsize recovery is a multifaceted process that begins well before any potential capsizing event:

1. Preparation and Setup for Intentional Capsizing

- *Gear Securing*: Prior to departure, all equipment must be securely tied down using standard operating procedures to prevent loss under turbulent conditions.
- *Safety Protocols*: Rangers are required to wear the designated waterborne uniform, ensuring quick adaptability to water immersion, including serviceable noninflatable life vests.
- *Role Assignments*: Specific crew members are designated for roles during the capsize drill, ensuring efficiency and safety throughout the exercise.

2. Conducting the Capsize

- *Initiation*: Upon the coxswain's command, designated Rangers will execute the capsize by strategically positioning and leveraging their body weight.
- *Execution*: As the boat capsizes, Rangers not involved in the initial tip-over will assist by grabbing onto pre-determined handles or fixtures to expedite the flipping process.

3. Recovery from Capsizing

- *Reorientation*: Rangers inside the boat utilize capsize lines attached to strategic points to right the vessel.
- *Reboarding*: All team members systematically re-enter the boat, starting with those designated to stabilize the craft post-capsize.

4. Post-Recovery Procedures

- *Equipment Check*: Immediate inventory checks are conducted to ensure all gear is accounted for and secure.
- *Continuation of the Mission*: After confirming the headcount and equipment status, the coxswain reinitiates the mission, guiding the team back into operational mode.

This part not only describes the stages involved in a controlled capsize and recovery drill, but it also emphasizes the necessity of planning, precision execution, and the duties that each Ranger must play. These aspects are critical for keeping the unit operationally ready and effective in the face of adversity. The exhaustive, step-by-step analysis guarantees that each Ranger is fully prepared to deal with real-world circumstances in an efficient and safe manner.

River Navigation and Movement

To effectively navigate rivers, you must first comprehend their unique characteristics. Each river characteristic—be it bends, stretches, sloughs, or sandbars—is critical in tactical decision-making and operational planning. Recognizing these characteristics aids in anticipating changes in the environment that may influence mobility and tactics.

- **Bends**: Sharp turns in the river that may require precise steering to navigate safely.
- **Reaches**: Straight segments between bends which may offer faster travel and easier navigation but less cover.
- **Sloughs**: Dead-end channels that can serve as hiding spots or tactical pitfalls if not recognized.
- **Sandbars**: Shallow areas that could pose hazards to navigation but might also serve as strategic points for concealment or operations.

Navigation Techniques

Effective river navigation requires specialized equipment and tried-and-true methods. Ensuring that each boat is equipped with the necessary navigational tools—such as compasses, GPS devices, and maps—is fundamental.

- **Compass and GPS Use**: For maintaining orientation and ensuring accurate movement along the planned route.
- **Map Reading**: Utilizing topographical and photo maps to understand the geographical layout and identify critical features of the river.

The success of river navigation is also dependent on clearly defined roles within the boat team:

- **Navigator**: Responsible for maintaining the route and providing direction using navigational tools. This individual must keep the map oriented and provide real-time updates to the observer.
- **Observer**: Works in tandem with the navigator, confirming visual landmarks and assisting in course adjustments based on real-time observations.

Movement Formations and Tactics

The formation of boats during river movements is strategically chosen to optimize speed, control, and security based on the specific mission requirements and river conditions. Common formations include:

- **Wedge**: Ideal for maximizing forward visibility and defensive potential.
- **Line**: Used for broad coverage of the river, suitable for maximizing firepower across the width of the river.
- **File**: Effective for narrow passages, minimizing the profile against threats from the riverbanks.
- **Echelon and Vee**: Useful in situations requiring a balance of speed and security, allowing for quick directional changes and concentration of firepower in a specific direction.

Several factors influence the choice of formation:

- **Tactical Needs**: Based on the mission objectives and the threat level.
- **River Conditions**: Adjustments are done based on the river's breadth, the presence of barriers, and the intensity of the stream.
- **Visibility and Cover**: Daytime operations might favor more open formations, whereas night operations may require tighter formations to maintain unit cohesion.

By understanding and applying these detailed navigation and movement strategies, Rangers can enhance their effectiveness in waterborne operations, ensuring they maintain tactical advantages and operational security in riverine environments.

Secure Landing Operations

Ensuring the security of a landing site is paramount in maintaining the safety and effectiveness of operations. Methods vary based on reconnaissance data, threat assessment, and tactical requirements:

- **Pre-landing Reconnaissance**: Utilizing scout swimmers or drones to survey the landing area for enemy presence and environmental hazards.

- **Establishing Over-watch Positions**: Deploying sharpshooters or surveillance teams in over-watch positions to monitor and secure the landing area from a distance.

Adapting to the operational environment requires flexibility in planning and execution:

- **Unsecured Landings**: Often necessary when immediate action is required. Procedures focus on rapid deployment and securing the area from threats as quickly as possible.
- **Secured Landings**: Preferable when time and conditions allow. Involves the detailed setup of defensive positions and thorough reconnaissance to ensure complete control over the landing zone.

Execution of Secure Landing

The execution of a secure landing is meticulously planned to adapt to varying operational and environmental conditions:

- **Standard Procedure**: Involves the systematic approach of units to the landing site, maintaining formation integrity and readiness to respond to threats.
- **Night Operations**: Special considerations such as the use of infrared and night vision equipment to maintain stealth and ensure effective landings under limited visibility.

Effective landing operations are characterized by seamless coordination and constant communication:

- **Coordination with Naval and Air Units**: Ensuring that timing and support are synchronized to provide cover and evacuation if necessary.
- **Use of Communication Equipment**: Implementing secure communication methods to maintain silence and operational security. This includes hand signals, encrypted radios, and other non-verbal communication tools.

Once the landing is executed, immediate actions are taken to consolidate the gain and prepare for further operations:

- **Security Setup**: Quick establishment of perimeter defenses to fend off potential counterattacks.
- **Equipment and Personnel Check**: Rapid inventory checks to ensure all critical equipment and personnel are accounted for and ready for the next phase of the operation.

These structured procedures and detailed planning ensure that Rangers can effectively secure and utilize landing sites in hostile environments, maintaining tactical superiority and operational momentum.

Quartering Party Operations

The quartering party plays a crucial role in pre-emptively securing and preparing landing sites to facilitate the smooth execution of waterborne operations:

- **Strategic Importance**: Understanding the quartering party's role in mitigating risks and ensuring the operational area is tactically advantageous before the arrival of the main body.
- **Logistical and Tactical Preparations**: Detailed briefing on the area's topographical and enemy intelligence, and equipping the quartering party with necessary tools and security equipment.

The early deployment is critical in establishing control and readiness at the landing site:

- **Timing and Insertion**: Coordinating the timing of the deployment to maximize operational security and efficiency.
- **Reconnaissance and Security Measures**: Conducting thorough reconnaissance of the landing site, establishing initial security measures, and providing real-time updates back to the main body.

Operational Procedures

The technical aspects of preparing for the main body's arrival are essential for ensuring the integrity and readiness of waterborne assets:

- **Equipment Rigging**: Detailed instructions on securing equipment within the boats to prevent loss or damage during deployment.
- **Lashing Techniques**: Utilizing advanced knotting and securing methods to ensure that all gear is tightly fastened and accessible for quick deployment.

Effective integration of the main body with the quartering party is essential for maintaining momentum and operational integrity upon arrival:

- **Communication Protocols**: Establishing robust communication links between the quartering party and the main body to ensure seamless integration and immediate operational readiness.
- **Landing and Reorganization Procedures**: Coordinating the precise landing sequences, immediate security setup, and the distribution of personnel and materials to prepared positions.

After the main body's arrival, the quartering party assists in the final setup and conducts an assessment to ensure operational goals are met:

1. **Final Security Sweeps**: Ensuring that the landing site is secure and all perimeter defenses are established.
2. **Operational Debrief**: Conducting a quick debrief to assess the success of the landing and the effectiveness of the quartering party, addressing any immediate concerns before proceeding with the mission.

These detailed preparations and procedures underscore the quartering party's pivotal role in enhancing the effectiveness and safety of waterborne operations, ensuring that Rangers maintain a tactical advantage from the moment of arrival.

CHAPTER 13: ADVANCED EMERGENCY MEDICAL RESPONSE

EMERGENCY MEDICAL TECHNIQUES

In the difficult environment of military operations, especially for Rangers operating in isolated or hazardous areas, the timely availability of medical personnel is not always assured. As a result, all Rangers must be adept in first aid. Emergency medical treatments can dramatically improve the outcome of combat injuries by stabilizing the injured until they can be safely transported to a medical institution. This chapter gives extensive instruction on the critical first aid methods that Rangers must understand in order to appropriately address life-threatening injuries.

The aftermath of an injury in a combat setting is essential and can be chaotic. The capacity to perform under fire necessitates not just courage, but also a high level of first aid knowledge. Each Ranger must be capable of handling this dual responsibility: continuing to combat the enemy while also giving medical care to wounded.

Initial Actions Under Fire
1. **Situational Awareness and Returning Fire**: The first goal is always to ensure the safety of the unit. Effective engagement with the adversary can give the required cover for dealing with casualties. Rangers are trained to retain their composure and focus, ensuring their return fire is controlled and effective, allowing them to respond to injured teammates.
2. **Casualty Assessment**: Quickly assessing the casualty's status is critical. The examination under fire focuses on detecting life-threatening injuries, particularly those that can result in breathing obstruction, uncontrolled bleeding, or tension pneumothorax. Rangers are taught to complete this assessment quickly in order to establish the casualty's immediate needs.
3. **Moving the Casualty to Cover**: The next step is to transport the casualty to a safer area, usually under cover, where additional assessment and treatment can be administered. This movement must be performed with caution to avoid further harm. Depending on the state of the casualty and the terrain, techniques like the fireman's carry or the use of an improvised stretcher may be required.
4. **Controlling Severe Bleeding**: Controlling hemorrhages is a top priority in trauma care. Rangers utilize tourniquets, wound packing, and pressure dressings to control bleeding. Training stresses the proper application of tourniquets above the wound site—usually two to three inches above a bleeding wound on a limb but not over a joint.

9-Line MEDEVAC Request
Safe evacuation from the battlefield is crucial for badly injured personnel. Rangers are taught to swiftly transmit a 9-line MEDEVAC request, which includes specifics such as location, radio frequency, number of casualties, special equipment required, and security at the pickup point. This communication must be clear and succinct in order to facilitate a timely medical response.

Casualty Feeder Card
This paperwork ensures a smooth transition of treatment from battlefield first responders to medical personnel. The casualty feeder card provides specific information regarding the casualty's injuries, treatment, and vital signs. This card tracks the casualty throughout the evacuation process, ensuring continuity of treatment.

Airway Management and Breathing Support
Effective airway management is pivotal in trauma care, particularly in battlefield settings where airway obstruction can quickly lead to fatality. Rangers are trained in both manual and instrumental techniques to secure a

casualty's airway.

Manual Airway Management Techniques
- **Chin Lift Method**: This approach is typically utilized when no spinal injuries are suspected. The rescuer puts one hand on the casualty's forehead and softly pulls backward. With the other hand, the rescuer reaches under the chin and elevates it, tilting the head back and pulling the tongue forward to clear the airway.
- **Jaw Thrust Method**: When a neck or spinal injury is feared, the jaw thrust approach is more secure. Kneeling above the casualty's head, place two fingers on each side of the lower jaw at an angle, and raise with both hands to pull the jaw forward. This approach does not move the cervical spine while attempting to expose the airway.

Instrumental Airway Management
1. **Nasal Airway Insertion (NPA)**: A nasopharyngeal airway is inserted into the nostril to keep the air passage open. It is generally well-tolerated by semi-conscious or unconscious patients without gag reflexes and is effective in providing a clear passage for air.
2. **Oral Airway Insertion (OPA)**: An oropharyngeal airway is used in unconscious people to keep the tongue from blocking the epiglottis and restricting the airway. To avoid mouth and throat injuries, this item should be properly sized and inserted.

These procedures and instruments are critical in successfully managing airway emergencies, ensuring that the patient has the best chance of maintaining adequate ventilation.

Breathing issues in trauma patients can swiftly progress to respiratory arrest if not handled immediately. Rangers are trained to assess and intervene effectively. Breathing assessment is an essential component of a trauma patient's initial examination. Signs of poor breathing include unusually quick or slow breathing, gasping, wheezing, or the difficulty to speak in complete words. Such indications require prompt attention.

- **Managing Chest Wounds**: Chest wounds, particularly sucking chest wounds, are a major challenge on the battlefield. Rangers use occlusive dressings to seal the wound and keep air from entering the thoracic cavity, which might result in a collapsed lung (pneumothorax).
- **Positioning the Casualty**: Proper posture can greatly improve a casualty's breathing. If the casualty is conscious, they should be placed in their most comfortable posture, which is usually sitting up. If unconscious, positioning depends on the injury. In the absence of spinal injuries, laying the victim on their side (recovery position) can aid in maintaining an open airway and facilitating breathing.

Circulation and Bleeding Control
In battlefield conditions, controlling severe bleeding is crucial and often life-saving. Rapid action to stop hemorrhage reduces the risk of shock and death.

Applying Tourniquets:
1. **Selection and Placement**: Use a Combat Application Tourniquet (CAT) or similar device. Put the tourniquet two to three inches over the wound, yet not above a joint. The location should be as proximal as possible on the injured limb.
2. **Tightening**: Squeeze the self-adhering band hard and reattach it to itself. Rotate the windlass till the bleeding has ended. To keep the tourniquet tight, secure the windlass.
3. **Documentation**: Mark the time of application on the tourniquet itself if possible.

Pressure Dressings:
Application: If a tourniquet is not necessary or practical, apply direct pressure with a hemostatic dressing if

available. Wrap the dressing tightly around the wound to apply constant pressure.

Maintenance: Continuously monitor the pressure dressing to ensure it remains tight and effective at controlling bleeding. Adjust as necessary, especially if the casualty must be moved.

Shock Management
Shock, particularly hemorrhagic shock, is a common and life-threatening condition following significant blood loss. Immediate recognition and management are vital to improve survival rates.

Identification of Shock Symptoms:
- Symptoms may include chilly, clammy skin, quick yet weak pulse, rapid breathing, decreased urine production, and confusion or loss of consciousness.
- Initial Assessment: Check for pale or bluish skin, especially around the lips and fingernails, which indicates poor blood circulation.

Immediate Interventions to Manage Shock:
1. **Control Bleeding**: Continuously monitor and control all sources of bleeding. Reapply or adjust tourniquets and pressure dressings as needed.
2. **Airway Management**: Ensure the airway is clear so that the casualty can receive maximum oxygen, which is crucial during shock.
3. **Fluid Replacement**: If trained and authorized, initiate intravenous (IV) fluids to replace lost blood volume. Use isotonic solutions like normal saline or lactated Ringer's if available.
4. **Positioning**: To promote venous return to the heart, lay the victim flat with legs elevated, unless other injuries prevent this. If the casualty is conscious and struggling to breathe, adjust to the most comfortable position to aid in respiration.

Continually reassess the casualty's condition, checking vital signs and consciousness levels. Adjust interventions based on changes in the casualty's status and prepare for evacuation to a higher echelon of care as soon as possible.

Management of Specific Injuries
Handling Extremity Injuries
1. **Assessment**: Prior to splinting, assess the injured extremity for breaks, deformities, tenderness, swelling, and the presence of a pulse distal to the injury to ensure continued circulation.
2. **Splint Application**: Use materials at hand such as sticks, magazines, or ready-made splints. Block the joints over and under the injured area without attempting to reposition the limb.
3. **Securing the Splint**: Wrap bandages around the splint and limb securely but ensure it's not so tight as to cut off circulation. Recheck for distal pulses after applying the splint to ensure blood flow is not compromised.

Abdominal Injuries
- **Immediate Action**: Do not attempt to push any protruding organs back into the abdominal cavity. Cover them with sterile saline-soaked gauze and a clean occlusive material to keep the area moist and reduce contamination.
- **Positioning**: Place the casualty in a supine position with knees bent (if not contraindicated by other injuries) to reduce abdominal muscle tension and pain.

Burn Care
- **Safety First**: Ensure that the casualty is removed from the cause of the burn. Quickly extinguish any flames or stop the casualty's contact with electrical sources.

- **Clothing and Jewelry Removal**: Carefully remove any clothing around the burn area. Cut clothing if necessary to avoid pulling over the burn. Remove jewelry and watches that can constrict swelling tissues.
- **Covering Burns**: Use sterile dressings or clean cloths to loosely cover the burns. Do not use ointments, creams, or ice. Burns should be kept dry and sterile to prevent infection.

GLOSSARY OF TERMS

1. **ABCs of First Aid**: Airway, Breathing, Circulation.
2. **Airway Adjuncts**: Devices used to maintain an open airway.
3. **Belay**: A method of securing a climber using a rope.
4. **Bend (River)**: A curve in the river.
5. **BTC (Bridge Team Commander)**: The leader responsible for the construction and management of a rope bridge.
6. **CASEVAC**: Casualty Evacuation.
7. **Chin Lift**: A method to open the airway by lifting the chin.
8. **CO2 Inflatable Life Preserver**: A life jacket that inflates using carbon dioxide cartridges.
9. **Combat Power**: The complete amount of destructive and/or disruptive force that a military unit/formation can use against its opponent at any given time.
10. **Coxswain**: The person responsible for navigating and piloting a boat.
11. **CRRC (Combat Rubber Raiding Craft)**: A lightweight, inflatable boat used by military for covert operations.
12. **Dead Water**: Water in a river with little to no current, often filled with debris.
13. **Debarkation**: The process of unloading personnel or equipment from a ship or aircraft.
14. **Distal Pulse**: A pulse taken far from the heart, typically used to check circulation in a limb.
15. **Echelon Formation**: A staggered, diagonal formation used by military units.
16. **Embarkation**: The process of loading personnel or equipment onto ships or aircraft.
17. **Farside**: The side of an obstacle (like a river) opposite the starting point.
18. **Feeder Card**: A form used in the military to document a casualty's condition.
19. **File Formation**: A single-column formation used by soldiers or vehicles.
20. **FLC (Field Load Carrier)**: Gear worn by soldiers to carry equipment in the field.
21. **Intravenous Therapy**: The administration of liquid chemicals straight into a vein.
22. **Jaw Thrust**: A method to open the airway without moving the neck.
23. **KIAs**: Killed In Action.
24. **Landing Site**: The area where troops are unloaded from transport, particularly in amphibious or air operations.
25. **Line Formation**: A formation where troops or vehicles form a straight line.
26. **MEDEVAC**: Medical Evacuation.
27. **Nasal Airways**: A tube placed into the nostrils to keep the airway open.
28. **Navigator**: A person responsible for planning the route or course of travel.
29. **Nearside**: The side of an obstacle closest to the starting point.
30. **Occlusive Dressing**: A kind of dressing that makes an airtight seal.
31. **Oral Airways**: A device placed in the mouth to keep the airway open.
32. **Patrolling**: The act of moving about an area to monitor or protect it.
33. **Poncho Raft**: A makeshift raft made using military ponchos.
34. **Pressure Dressing**: A dressing applied tightly to control bleeding.
35. **PSG (Platoon Sergeant)**: The senior non-commissioned officer in a platoon.
36. **Quartering Party**: A group that moves ahead to secure and prepare an area for the main body.
37. **Reach (River)**: A straight section of a river.
38. **Reconnaissance**: A mission to collect information using visual observation or other detecting techniques.
39. **Rope Bridge**: A makeshift bridge constructed using ropes.
40. **Sandbar**: A sand or coarse sediment ridge that is either submerged or partially exposed.

41. Secure Landing: Operations designed to secure a landing area before the arrival of the main forces.

42. Shock: A serious condition characterized by decreased blood flow to the body's tissues.

43. Slough: A side channel or an inlet on a river, often stagnant.

44. Sniper Position: A concealed location from which a sniper can observe or fire at targets.

45. Splint: A device intended to immobilize a body portion and avoid future harm.

46. Tourniquet: A device used to constrict blood arteries and stop excessive blood flow.

47. VEE Formation: A formation shaped like a "V" used by military units.

48. Wedge Formation: A V-shaped formation used especially when advancing against an opponent.

49. Work Vest: A type of life jacket or flotation device used during operational activities.

50. 9-Line MEDEVAC Request: A standardized format to request a medical evacuation.

Made in the USA
Columbia, SC
07 January 2025

51233990R00057